NINE
EMPOWERING
SECRETS OF
SUCCESSFUL
LIVING

Denis Waitley

Thomas Nelson Publishers

Nashville • Atlanta • London • Vancouver

Published in Nashville, Tennessee, by Thomas Nelson, Inc., Publishers, and distributed in Canada by Word Communications, Ltd., Richmond, British Columbia.

The Bible version used in this publication is THE NEW KING JAMES VERSION. Copyright © 1979, 1980, 1982, Thomas Nelson, Inc., Publishers.

ISBN 0-8407-9685-4

Printed in the United States of America

1 2 3 4 5 6 — 99 98 97 96 95 94

CONTENTS

Planning for the Whole of You

THE BOOK you hold in your hand is more than a goal-setting book. It is a book that will enable you to design and implement a life plan.

A plan is a goal that is set in time—a detailed and systematic approach to achieving a goal that is practical and precise. Plans involve calendars, deadlines, and points at which rewards are reaped.

In a number of ways, this book is *not* a book. It is, rather, an educational experience. It calls on you to learn new things about yourself and to push yourself to explore some new ideas and opinions that you may never have encountered. As such, this book gives you direction for learning, but you alone can do the ultimate learning and subsequent planning. This book provides structure, which in turn calls for you to focus your thoughts, opinions, and feelings on certain areas of your life, but you alone will draw conclusions based on *your* responses. In the end, this book will be of *your own creation*.

At the outset, you are asked to face several facts about the experience that lies ahead for you.

■ The Honesty Factor

This book cannot be more honest than you will be with yourself. Your honesty in facing yourself is critical to the integrity of the plans you make. If you make plans based on who you hope you are or who you think others desire you to be, your plans will be forged on faulty premises. You must deal with the elements of this book truthfully if you are going to develop a life plan that is of substance and quality with enduring and eternal characteristics.

■ The Intensity of Introspection

This book represents an intense experience. There is no way that you can complete this book in one sitting. Or in one day. Or perhaps even in one week. Give yourself a season of planning.

Where there is no revelation, the people cast off restraint.
—Proverbs 29:18

Make time to spend with this book. Set aside part of each day—or week—to work on the elements here. If you need to, get up and take a walk in the middle of a segment. Clear your mind of extraneous thoughts and your schedule of annoying interruptions. Gain a focus. And dig deep within yourself.

Introspection is sometimes dangerous work. There are dangers in any kind of mining, and to a great extent, you will be mining your inner depths. Don't be afraid of your fears. Don't take pride in your praises. The more you honestly face up to who you are, what you want, when you want it, and how you intend to go about getting it, the more in focus the big picture of your life is going to become.

The process of this book requires energy. There may be many times when you feel that you've done enough planning—answered enough questions, made enough lists—and be tempted to give up. Take a break, but then come back when you feel physically and mentally refreshed. Keep working and keep learning. Don't give up halfway through this process.

■ Searching for Significance

At the end of each chapter, you will be asked to write summary statements. As you prepare to write them, look for optimal significance in what you have written in previous segments of the chapter.

Ask yourself questions: Why did I write what I did? Why do I want what I want? How much do I want what I say I want? What about the discrepancies between what I say and what I do? Why isn't my life more consistent in this area? These are tough questions. Finding their answers can be one of the most significant exercises of your entire life.

D r e a m i n '

Your mental picture of yourself is the key to your healthy development. You are the writer, director, and star of either an Oscar-winning epic or a Grade B movie. *Who you see in your imagination will always rule your world.*

You are also your greatest critic. You can devastate your self-esteem and creativity with sarcastic and negative reviews of your daily performance. Or you can elevate your self-image with encouraging and positive feedback and previews of coming attractions. When you're talking to yourself, watch your language!

Here are some of the statements that I have found most helpful in opening myself up to new dreams and new creative ideas. I speak these phrases aloud several times and then let my mind begin to "see" good, positive behavior that depicts the phrase.

My breathing is relaxed and effortless, my heartbeat is slow and regular, my muscles are relaxed and warm, I am relaxed and at peace . . .

I am a unique and special creation of God . . . and I'd rather be me than anyone else in the world . . .

Now is the best time in the history of the world to be alive . . .

I give the best of me . . .

I keep the commitments I make and earn the respect of others . . .

All is well with me now . . .

My world is opening and expanding . . .

I relish each golden day . . .

I take time for sunsets and flowers . . .

I am gentle and giving to my loved ones . . .

I am strong and vital . . .

I take time for older people . . .

I take time to play like a child . . .

I am being made whole . . .

I help other people become winners . . .

Today is the best day ever . . .

I thank God for the gift of life . . .

—Seeds of Greatness

■ The Quest for Wholeness

Ultimately, this book is designed in hopes that you will use it as a tool toward gaining greater wholeness and balance in your life. These two concepts— wholeness and balance—are at the heart of all that you hold in your hands.

Wholeness is health, unity, sufficiency, and the peace that comes from having enough of everything you need in your life. Balance is having the various parts of your life in proper proportion to each other. The two terms are vitally interrelated. Success, by definition for this book, is "balanced wholeness."

Throughout the book, you will see an illustration representing your life.

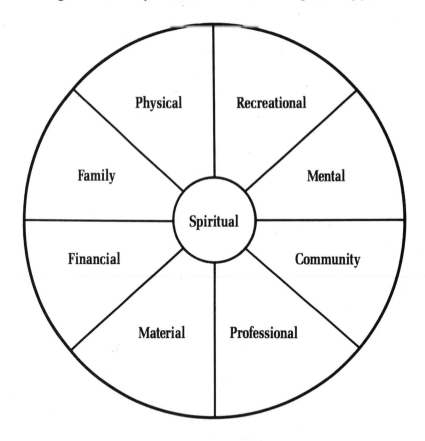

You will note that there are eight components and a core. At the core of your life is your spirit. It is not just one aspect of your life—it is the very nature of who you are. All of your dreams and goals and plans must flow from it. For that reason, we begin with an exploration of your spiritual self and then move outward to explore the physical, family, financial, material, professional, community, mental, and recreational components.

These components are not in any order of priority. If you desire to complete these chapters in an order other than what is provided here, do so. Each of these areas of your life is vital to your wholeness. Each one should be seen as a whole, even as we discuss its secret.

Each of the "nine empowering secrets" is a statement at the beginning of each chapter representing the essence of that chapter. For example, the first empowering secret is represented by the statement: "You are not a human being having spiritual experiences. You are a spiritual being having human experiences." It is the guidepost for all that follows in its particular chapter. By understanding that all of your behaviors and actions are a manifestation of your spiritual core, you will be able to place the emphasis in your life planning by applying that secret of seeking to identify and do the most important things first.

As you approach each of the nine secrets, ask yourself the questions: "Do I understand what this secret means to me in my personal life?" "Am I committed to making each secret a stepping stone in my daily activities?" If so, you will have achieved the main mission of this book, which is to turn the "nine empowering secrets" into nine personal revelations on successful living. When a secret is understood and revealed, it is a secret no more.

Gaining insight into the nine secrets discussed here will empower you to live successfully. As you work your way through this book, be alert to ways in which the components overlap. We may focus on one component of your life, but ultimately, we are talking about the whole you. Think in terms of wholeness as you dream, set goals, and make plans.

■ Why Plan?

Planning leads to action in a way that dreams and goals can't. A dream can give you something to aim at. A goal can tighten the focus of that dream and help you visualize it more fully, even as you direct your will toward the realization of that dream. A plan compels you to act.

Finding God's will and walking in it may be another way of stating "make a life plan." If you simply take life as it comes and never seek to conform your will to God's will or your ways to His ways, your life will meander without a strong sense of direction, purpose, or fulfillment.

The Lord isn't at all against our making plans. He's against our worshiping our plans, and He's against our making plans that leave Him out. To be more precise, we must ask the Lord to give us our plans.

The Lord calls on us to work, to do, to speak, and to think. He asks us to be His hands, eyes, feet, and mind on this earth. He calls on us to make decisions and to engage in activities that will extend His kingdom.

We ask and believe that God will reveal His desires to us and plant His dreams in us. We then make our goals based on the desires and dreams. We forge the goals into a plan, and we begin to work the plan so that a new reality is created. All along the way, we continually ask the Lord, "Am I on the right track? Am I pursuing this as quickly as You want it pursued? Am I becoming the person You want me to be?"

All of creation speaks to us that the Lord is a Lord of infinitely detailed plans. This universe runs according to precision and with harmony that is nearly unfathomable to our finite minds. Our God is a God of order. Part of the message to the early church was that the Spirit of God brings about harmony among people—there is a oneness, a wholeness, a balance to all that God does.

This is what you pursue in the life planner you hold. You are in search of God's wholeness and His balance for you. This is not a book intended to exalt the mind or draw you into a set of plans contrary to God's will. Quite the opposite! This is a book intended to draw you into a deeper relationship with the Lord and into God's plan for you. That will happen only if you see this book as a *spiritual* exercise. Approach each chapter with a heart open to the Lord and the question always in the back of your mind, "What is Your will, O Lord?"

> Come now, you who say, "Today or tomorrow we will go to such and such a city, spend a year there, buy and sell, and make a profit"; whereas you do not know what will happen tomorrow. For what is your life? It is even a vapor that appears for a little time and then vanishes away. Instead you ought to say, "If the Lord wills, we shall live and do this or that." But now you boast in your arrogance. All such boasting is evil.
> —James 4:13–16

■ A Starting Appraisal

Take another look at the illustration of your life introduced to you a few pages ago. Indicate for each component and the core where you believe you stand right now. Minus (–) means inadequate. Plus (+) represents ideal.

Spiritual	(–) . . . . (+)
Physical	(–) . . . . (+)
Family	(–) . . . . (+)

Financial	(–) . . . . (+)
Material	(–) . . . . (+)
Professional	(–) . . . . (+)
Community	(–) . . . . (+)
Mental	(–) . . . . (+)
Recreational	(–) . . . . (+)

No doubt you have scaled some aspects of your life lower than others. They are probably the areas in which you should begin to work after you have completed the chapter on the spiritual secret. No matter how high you ideally scaled yourself spiritually, begin with chapter 1.

■ Dreaming Unique God-Given Dreams

Among the first few pages of each chapter, you will find a page entitled "Dream a Little Dream." These pages are very possibly the most valuable ones of this book.

- Many people have lost their ability to dream, especially to dream about themselves. Dreams invite you to see a future that is better than the present. Dreams compel you to grow and to develop yourself in ways you haven't thus far. Dreams give you energy and enthusiasm.
- Dreams are closely linked to potential. What you *can't* imagine will very likely not happen. What you *can* imagine is very likely possible.
- You are called to dream by God. In fact, one of the promises made about the Holy Spirit is that He will enable people to envision God's "better ways and means."

The ability to visualize is a God-given ability. You need to use it in a godly way for godly purposes.

One of the best-kept secrets about the link between our bodies and our minds is that our minds can't tell the difference between real experiences and ones that are vividly and repeatedly imagined. When we visualize our success—truly seeing ourselves as whole men and women, living in balance within ourselves and in harmony with others and with nature—we create a pattern in our minds that leads us to make decisions on the basis of our success. In many ways, we *become* what we think, dream, hope, and imagine.

The apostle Paul wrote to the Ephesians, "Be renewed in the spirit of your mind" (Eph. 4:23). Paul had undergone such a transformation in his thought life, and he well understood that we need to change our old patterns of thinking to align them with the way Jesus would think and act. This renewal of your mind requires an ability to believe that it is *possible* for you to become a new creature in Christ, one who can make right decisions and live a pure and good life. That belief in possibility is dreaming!

If you are troubled by the idea of dreaming, especially dreaming about yourself, ask the Lord to guide your dreams and your imagination. Ask Him to reveal to you who He created you to be and how He wants you to think, dream, and imagine.

■ And So We Begin . . .

Take a deep breath. Swallow your fear and apprehension. And prepare to embark on one of the greatest journeys of your entire life—a journey that can lead you to the success you want.

Whether you know it today or not, whether you will admit it openly to yourself or not, you long to be made whole. That's the desire of every person—to be someone whose life is complete and in balance.

The journey toward wholeness beckons you from the first moment that you realize you *aren't* whole, that you aren't living up to your potential in Christ Jesus. The journey takes effort, but it is rewarding. And I can promise you this: it is never boring.

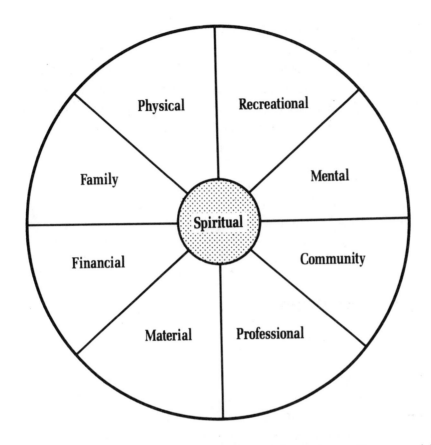

SECRET: You are not a human being having spiritual experiences. You are a spiritual being having human experiences.

SCRIPTURE: "If we live in the Spirit, let us also walk in the Spirit" (Gal. 5:25).

Seeking the Most Important Things First: The Spiritual Core

IN PLANNING for total success in life—which is wholeness, the attribute that Jesus desired for all men and women to have—you begin with your spiritual nature. The spirit has been put purposefully at the core of the illustration of your life. Your plans must flow from the inside out—and to be workable, worthy plans, they must flow from what you believe to be God's purpose for your life.

In this chapter, you will find several exercises and forms that can help you identify who you are and who you desire to be as God's unique creation. You are asked to reflect on the condition of your soul and to put into writing things that you may never have thought about, much less put into words or on paper. From the very opening pages of this book, you are undertaking the most difficult of tasks—deep and thoughtful appraisal of the most vulnerable, most sensitive, most mysterious aspect of your being. Take courage as you discover the spiritual secret.

The more you explore this area of your life, the more you will have a sense of priority that will spill over into all other areas of goal setting. Unless this area of the spirit comes first—in your thinking now and, ultimately, as you live out your life plans—you will not be able to fill your unique place in life or accomplish the unique tasks the Lord God has ordained for you to accomplish with maximum effectiveness, efficiency, and reward. Begin at the core of your being. Find yourself there. All other lists and ideas will flow from your knowledge of your place in God's kingdom and your moment in God's eternity.

Jesus said it best: "Seek first the kingdom of God and His righteousness, and all these things shall be added to you" (Matt. 6:33).

■ Your Spiritual Identity

Most of us know who we are in the flesh. We are "the son of Jim and Joan" or "the daughter of Sam and Sally." We grow up knowing our names, our addresses and phone numbers, and certain key facts about ourselves.

This form provides an outline for you to use in constructing a *spiritual* resume. What other factors might you include if you were trying to tell someone who you are as a spiritual creation?

Completing a Spiritual Resume

My Spiritual Resume

Name: _____

Date (year or age) of spiritual birth (see John 3:1–16): _____

Date of water baptism (see Acts 8:18; 10:47–48): _____

Date of receiving the gift of God's Spirit (see Acts 8:15): _____

Primary spiritual role in serving God's people: _____

_____

_____

The New Testament writers identified five primary leadership roles in the early church. (1) *Apostles* were trailblazers, ones sent out to pioneer new works, new missions, or new emphases in the spreading of the gospel. (2) *Prophets* preached the Word of God in its fullness and had a spiritual understanding of the full breadth and depth of God's purposes and His work on the earth (including an ability to perceive future or impending events and situations). (3) *Evangelists* went about telling others about the good news of Jesus Christ and what He did and does for His people. (4) *Teachers* taught the Scriptures to others. (5) *Pastors* nurtured the body of Christ and brought it to greater wholeness (generally through prayer, counseling, and operation of spiritual gifts related to healing, deliverance, and administration).

Some people profoundly exemplify one of these gifts; others sometimes operate in two roles to greater or lesser extents. Nearly all church work tends to flow out of one of these roles. A Sunday school teacher is an example of a teacher; a person who delivers meals to those newly home from the hospital fulfills a pastoral

DREAM A LITTLE DREAM:
At Home in the Throne Room of Heaven

Take a few minutes to imagine yourself walking up the steps to God's throne room in heaven. You pass through the entryway to find yourself in His very presence—surrounded by saints and angels, in a room filled with the most glorious music, sights, sounds, and aromas you have ever experienced. You have been cleansed by the Lord Himself, and you stand freely in His presence.

Imagine yourself there! What is this experience like? What captures your attention and elicits your awe? What do you say? What does He say to you? What are your concerns? Who are you in Him? Who is He in you? What matters? What does He say about your nature, your efforts, your dreams and goals?

Write freely as thoughts and images come to your mind:

_____

_____

_____

_____

_____

_____

_____

_____

_____

_____

_____

_____

_____

_____

_____

_____

_____

_____

_____

_____

_____

_____

_____

_____

_____

role; a person who eagerly invites others to attend church or church-related func-tions is an evangelist; founder-leaders of new churchwide outreaches or ministry programs function in an apostolic manner.

My spiritual giftedness: _____

The New Testament lists a number of "gifts of the Holy Spirit." (See 1 Cor. 12:7–10 and Romans as examples.) These are gifts *of* the Holy Spirit, not limited to the traits of a person and not the permanent property of a person. The Holy Spirit flows *through* Christians to manifest these gifts for the spiritual profit of another person and the whole body of Christ. Most people seem to manifest one or more of these gifts more than they do others. Among the gifts listed in the New Testament are the ones below. Check off those that you believe have applied or do apply to you:

☐ Word of wisdom   ☐ Word of knowledge
☐ Faith   ☐ Gift of healing
☐ Working of miracles   ☐ Prophecy
☐ Discerning of spirits   ☐ Different kinds of tongues
☐ Administration   ☐ Interpretation of tongues
☐ Intercessory prayer   ☐ Leadership
☐ Ministry to needy   ☐ Exhortation
☐ Giving   ☐ Hospitality
☐ Acts of mercy   ☐ Other: _____
                            _____

The foremost spiritual experiences of my life include

_____
_____
_____
_____
_____
_____

The main ways in which the Lord has led me to serve others through the years have been

_____

_____

_____

_____

_____

The body (or bodies) of believers with whom the Lord has called me to be a part (your denomination or religious affiliation as well as other ministry groups you feel compelled to support):

_____

_____

_____

The spiritual gifts and experiences of God that I would love to experience in my life:

_____

_____

_____

I would describe the current state of my soul, or my current spiritual development, as being

_____

_____

_____

These are the ways I can see that my spiritual life has changed during the last five years:

_____

_____

_____

These are the ways in which I would like for my spiritual life to change during the coming five years:

_____

_____

_____

These are changes I desire to see made in my spiritual life immediately or in the very near future:

_____

_____

_____

_____

Writing Your Epitaph or Eulogy

A meaningful exercise is to write out your epitaph—what you would like placed on your tombstone—and then to write out your eulogy or plan your funeral service (including eulogy, sermon, and choices of music, Scriptures, flowers, and so forth).

My Epitaph

Limit yourself to twenty-five words:

_____

_____

_____

My Eulogy

You don't need to write this out in prose form. Note words or phrases that you would most like to have as the hallmarks of your eulogy. What do you want people truly to know or remember about you?

_____

_____

_____

_____

My Memorial Service

What would you like done at a memorial service, wake, or party in your remembrance? Note such things as your favorite words, songs, flowers, and other meaningful symbols or acts that you would like to see done as your friends and loved ones remember you after your death. (Don't approach this exercise with dread. Think of it as a celebration. Reflect on what you write. Are you living the life that will result in those accolades? Do others really know what you believe, what you consider to be important, or what you count as beautiful? Reflect on what more you might do to convey the real you, the inner you.)

_____

_____

_____

_____

_____

_____

_____

Spiritual Attributes

The Scriptures use a number of metaphors to describe God's people:

salt	light	leaven
sheep	pillar	branch (of the vine)
clay	garden	building
bride	child	tree

He [Jesus] said to her, "Daughter, be of good cheer; your faith has made you well. Go in peace." —Luke 8:48

Other words describe a person's perceived relationship with the Lord:

follower	disciple	the redeemed of the Lord
healed	saved	the called
His body	seeker	the church
the lost	the found	the cleansed
faithful	chosen	the righteous

A number of metaphors are also used to describe Jesus Christ, and resulting metaphors about His followers can be made from them. For example, Jesus is called the Rock of our salvation. One person described himself as a "piece of the Rock." Here are a few of the metaphors and words used to describe Jesus:

Way	Savior	Morning Star
Light	Rose of Sharon	Firm Foundation
Teacher	Balm of Gilead	Supreme Sacrifice
Messiah	True Vine	Cleft in the Rock
Master	Bridegroom	Prince of Peace
Counselor	Eternal One	Alpha and Omega
Shepherd	Pearl of Great Price	

Reflect on these words. Add others in each area as you think of them.

What are the seven metaphors or words that have the most meaning for you in describing the Lord?

_____

_____

What are the seven metaphors or words that have the most meaning for you in describing yourself and your relationship with God?

_____

_____

For which metaphors or words do you find that you have very little meaning or understanding? (These may be good areas for you to pursue in study or reflection.)

_____

_____

The Struggle

Most people who search for a deeper spiritual meaning in life have struggled in the process. The apostle Paul spoke of an ongoing war that he experienced in his life between "the lusts of the flesh" and the "desires of his heart." In Romans 7:19, we read these poignant words of confession: "For the good that I will to do, I do not do; but the evil I will not to do, that I practice."

Much of our struggle can come into focus when we face up to the things that we are battling and name them for the sin that they are. Galatians 5:19–21 provides a list of "the works of the flesh." Other besetting sins are described elsewhere in Scripture. The list below is not comprehensive, but it may give you a start in identifying what you are battling in the deepest recesses of your soul:

adultery	greed
pride	outbursts of wrath
lust	lewdness
uncleanness	dissensions
selfish ambitions	heresies
gossip	envy
idolatry	murderous spirit
sorcery	drunkenness
hatred	critical spirit

contention	darkness/evil oppression
revelries	poor stewardship
besetting worry	dishonest dealings
idleness	jealousy
lying	other: _____
fornication	_____

What do you consider to be your foremost inner enemy? Of what do you find yourself most desiring to be cleansed, forgiven, or freed?

_____

_____

The good news of the gospel is that we can be transformed in the inner being and be filled with God's presence, the Holy Spirit. Galatians 5:22–23 describes the attributes—the fruit—of God's Spirit at work in us. Reflect on these nine attributes:

love	kindness	longsuffering
joy	goodness	faithfulness
peace	gentleness	self-control

For which of these attributes do you desire to see an increase in your life?

_____

_____

■ Spiritual Nurturing

We must nurture our spirits and "feed" our spiritual nature, just as we feed our bodies to help them grow, stay healthy, and function with energy. Two types of spiritual food are described in the Scriptures. The first is the Word of God. It is called in various places the bread of life, the milk of the Word, the meat of the Word, and heavenly food. The other type of spiritual food is Jesus Christ Himself, who invites us to partake of His body and blood in Holy Communion and, in so doing, to become His very body that is active and alive in ministry on this earth.

Reflect on your spiritual nutritional plan, and ask yourself, What am I feeding my soul?

Feeding on the Word

Let's begin with two basic premises:

1. It's important for you to read the Bible—all of it. God's Word must be taken as a whole to truly understand how concepts are relevant to each other and how one teaching may be balanced by another.
2. It's important for you to read the Bible periodically. Ideally, that would be daily.

Just as with physical food, exactly what you eat, the amount you eat, and the time you spend eating are individual matters. Consider two approaches—one based on time and the other on amount.

A Plan Based on Time

How much time a day do you currently spend in reading God's Word?

_____

How much time a day do you *desire* to spend in reading God's Word?

_____

Is there an immediate increase you can take now in moving toward your ultimate goal? If so, how much time might you begin to spend each day in reading God's Word? (Don't set your ultimate goal or your intermediate goal too high. Set a goal that you realistically believe you can reach and maintain.)

_____

A Plan Based on Amount

You may want to set a goal for reading one book of the Bible a month or a specific number of chapters a day or week.

Developing Your Own Plan

The Old Testament has 39 books and 929 chapters. The New Testament has 27 books and 260 chapters. In all, the Bible has 66 books and 1,189 chapters (which breaks down to 3.25 chapters per day to complete reading the entire Bible in a year).

Many "through the Bible in a year" reading plans are available. They generally call for you to read a passage from the Old Testament and the New Testament each day—usually for a total of three to four chapters.

There are other plans you may want to consider:

- One plan suggests that you read something from the Old Testament, something from the Psalms, something from the Gospels (Matthew, Mark, Luke, and John), and something from the remaining portions of the New Testament each day. You may want to break this reading down into morning and evening segments.
- One plan suggests that Monday through Friday you read something from the Old Testament in the mornings (passage and book of your choice) and something from the New Testament in the evenings (again, of your choice), and that you focus on the Psalms over the weekend.
- One plan suggests that you begin with the Gospels and read them through three times in sequence before branching out into other books of the Bible.

Like a diet plan, each plan works to cover the whole of God's Word—if you will only work the plan!

My Plan for Reading the Whole of God's Word

Write the plan of your choice for reading the whole of God's Word:

_____

_____

_____

_____

Building a Bible Reference Library

As you read the Bible, you are likely to have questions about the people, places, customs, and historical context for various Bible stories. You'll want to develop a basic reference library. Begin with a concordance (to look up passages by topic or word) and a Bible dictionary. You may also find these materials helpful: a topical Bible (with passages broken down by topic), a Bible atlas, and Bible commentary books (by book of the Bible).

A number of study Bibles include concordances, dictionary information, and illuminating commentary, as well as maps, lists, and charts.

Even if you purchase one substantive Bible-related reference book a year, you'll soon have a quality library for researching your questions related to the Bible.

My Bible Library-Building Plan

Identify the books related to the Bible that you would like to add to your reference library, and indicate your anticipated date (or year) of purchase:

_____

_____

_____

_____

_____

Inspirational Reading

In addition to reading God's Word, read what others have said about God and about His Word. These writings are not substitutes for a direct reading of God's Word. They may, however, be useful in helping you understand God's Word and apply it to your life, and they may be a great source of inspiration. Such books include the following:

- Daily inspirational guides (these little booklets or books provide daily readings that generally include a verse of Scripture and perhaps a prayer along with a paragraph or two of teaching or anecdotal material)
- Books about one aspect of the spiritual journey, such as prayer, forgiveness, or healing
- Bible study books that focus on one topic or one book of the Bible, books about people in the Bible, or books that apply certain principles of the Bible to everyday life
- Journals and diaries or biographies of noteworthy spiritual leaders
- Hymnals and prayer books
- Books of poetry and reflection with godly themes

Another approach is to focus on one noteworthy Christian and read all that you can about that person or by that person. Is there someone who has captured your interest or about whom you would like to read or know more? Do you have a favorite Christian writer? Would you like to explore the writings of a person you have heard about but have never read? Name that person (or those persons) here:

_____

_____

Still another approach is to focus on a particular topic of interest and develop your own course of study, for example, an in-depth study on the life and ministry of Jesus, a book of the Bible, or a portion of church history.

My Inspirational Reading Plan

Identify authors, books, or subjects that you would like to study, and indicate a time frame for doing such a study:

_____

_____

_____

_____

_____

_____

Hearing God's Word

Romans 10:17 tells us that "faith comes by hearing, and hearing by the word of God." Do you have a plan for regularly "hearing" the Word of God? Something about the spoken word sinks deep within the spirit and stirs the soul. The spoken or sung word of God often triggers something in the spirit that isn't tapped when we read the Word of God silently and take it in through the filter of our minds.

List those from whom you regularly hear God's Word—either preached or taught. (Include those who preach from the pulpit at your church or teach your Sunday school class, radio or television programs, favorite singers, and tapes of sermon series.)

Jesus said to him, "If you can believe, all things are possible to him who believes." Immediately the father of the child cried out and said with tears, "Lord, I believe; help my unbelief!"
—Mark 9:23–24

_____

_____

_____

_____

_____

_____

Enthusiasm

Whether you are just getting back up on your horse or galloping away toward your goals of success, you need one vital emotion that is crucial to your journey: *enthusiasm.*

The term "enthusiasm" may sound phony to you. Too reminiscent of high school cheerleaders or corporate pep talks or "Uncle Tom" smiles to please the boss.

True enthusiasm, however, has very little to do with outward exuberance and very much to do with an inner fire.

The word "enthusiasm" stems from the Greek word "enthous," meaning "inspired." And the word "enthous" is derived from an even more ancient Greek word that combines "theos," which means "God," and "entos" meaning "within." So, the original use of the term "enthusiasm" literally means "the spirit of God within you."

God, who created all the beauty of this earth and in the heavens, who is the source of all goodness, truth, and love, is the Spirit who energizes you, encourages you, enriches you with the fervor to excel yourself. When you come to understand that God's spirit is always within, you'll be surprised by the joy and unbounded enthusiasm you have burning inside you.

—Denis Waitley and Reni L. Witt
The Joy of Working

Reflect on your list. Are you hearing a good balance? Is the whole of God's Word being covered? Are there areas that aren't being addressed?

_____

_____

My Plan for Hearing God's Word

What might you do to enhance your hearing of God's Word? Are there cassette series that you need to borrow or purchase? Is there a class, course, or study series that you might attend? Note your ideas:

_____

_____

_____

Feeding on the Lord Himself

People outside the early church sorely misunderstood its practices of "feeding" on Christ. Jesus told us to do this. We are regularly to partake of Him by faith, in our hearts, and with thanksgiving. In essence, we are to acknowledge Him at all times and in all places of our lives. We are to expect Him to be present with us. We are to rejoice and give praise for what He is doing in us and through us at all times.

There are several ways in which we call the Lord to our remembrance and concede the throne of our hearts to Him.

Holy Communion

Perhaps the foremost way through the ages has been the partaking of Holy Communion—taking the bread and cup that represent to us His body and blood. Ask yourself,

When was the last time I participated in a service of Holy Communion?

_____

What does Holy Communion mean to me?

_____

How often do I have a need for Holy Communion?

_____

What can I do to have that need met in my life?

_____

What results do I expect in my life for having partaken of Christ's body and blood?

_____

_____

Praise and Thanksgiving

Another way to call the Lord to remembrance and to focus attention on His presence is to offer praise and thanksgiving to Him. As we praise Him, we recount His qualities and character, and in the process, we come to realize anew our reliance on Him to be for us all that we cannot be or become in our own strength.

Don't limit your praises or your thanksgivings to things that seem lofty or ideal. Be practical. Think like a child. You may praise the Lord for having enough gravy for your mashed potatoes, the beautiful sunrise you saw this morning, fresh flowers from the garden, not capsizing your sailboat when you were caught by an unexpected storm, the birth of a new calf, and so forth. Nothing is too small or too large to offer as a phrase of praise or thanksgiving to God.

Your Praise List

Challenge yourself to list one hundred things for which you praise or thank the Lord. Use separate sheets of paper or a special notebook for this exercise.

Spending Time with the Lord

Don't limit yourself to reading, studying, hearing tapes or sermons, praising— all of which are very good and should be done, but all of which reflect a doing, doing, doing approach to God. Give yourself some time to "be" in God's presence:

- Take a walk with God. Let Him reveal to you things as you walk.
- Meditate quietly on His Word. Just sit and think back through what you've been reading from God's Word and in inspirational books.
- Think about yourself sitting in the throne room of God, watching all that you imagine to be said and done there.
- Think about yourself sitting on a park bench with God, not talking, but just sitting quietly, watching those around you and enjoying each other's presence.
- Think about yourself being cradled in God's arms, just as if you were a very young child. How would He hold you? How would you feel?

Developing a Relationship that Brings Inner Peace and Joy

For the Christian, a state of soul peace nearly always results from having a connection—of knowing and experiencing a close personal relationship—with the Lord God. Peace flows from relationship, not from something that you find within your isolated self. The amazing feature of this peace is a related joy.

Some people feel closer to God when they are in the mountains, far from city life. Others feel a closer connection to God when they are with children at play. Some feel closer as they sit in a cathedral.

Ask yourself,

Have I ever felt close to God? If so, when?

_____

Do I feel that I have a connection with God—a personal relationship with Him? If so, can I point to a time when that was established?

_____

If not, do I want such a relationship? Do I know how to go about having one?

_____

When have I felt closest to God (a specific time, place, or situation; once, periodically, or routinely)?

_____

Where do I most often go to find God or to feel close to Him?

_____

To what extent do I need beauty to feed my creativity or my soul? Where do I go to see, feel, or experience beauty?

_____

What evokes for me a sense of calm and order?

_____

What do I truly find satisfying?

_____

What gives me a sense of fulfilling my purpose in life?

_____

What gives me a sense that I am transcending time and space—that I've really had an eternal moment or done something that will last for all eternity?

_____

■ Spiritual Discipline

Some general spiritual disciplines have been recognized through the centuries: having a prayer life, serving others, keeping God's commandments, and sharing the good news about Jesus Christ with others. We'll take a look at each of the first three in the coming pages and the fourth in a later chapter.

Having a Prayer Life

Prayer is talking to God with a purpose in mind. Earlier, we talked about unstructured communication with the Lord—a time to praise, a time to hear, a time simply to "be" in His presence. Prayer is petitioning—asking things of God, asking on behalf of others (often called intercession), and confronting evil in the spiritual realm (often called spiritual warfare). Prayer is active, intentional, and very specific communication. The person who prays expects God to hear and respond for good.

Having a prayer life is making prayer a routine part of your spiritual journey. It means praying regularly, consistently, and persistently.

Answer these questions as honestly as you can:

How much time, on an average day, do I spend in prayer? _____

How much time do I feel I *should* spend each day in prayer? _____

If you don't spend as much time in prayer as you think you should, what might you do to take a step toward spending more time in prayer?

_____

_____

Why do you believe it's important to spend more time in prayer? Cite some specific reasons.

_____

_____

Appraising Your Prayer Life

Many people are troubled by prayer. They don't understand it, don't feel they know how to do it, or are afraid of its mystery. Reflect on some of your opinions and feelings about prayer. Do any of these responses fit how you feel?

exciting	true sense of purpose
boring	sense of accomplishment
dangerous	habit
responsibility	intimacy with God
rote	leads to worship
joyful	profound impact
hard work	other: _____
duty	_____

Answer these questions about prayer:

Why do I pray?

_____

What do I expect to get personally out of praying?

_____

What do I expect God to do as a result of my prayers?

_____

What role does my faith (or believing) play in my prayers?

_____

How do I feel as I get ready to pray?

_____

How do I feel while I am praying?

_____

How do I feel after I've prayed?

_____

How important is it for me to spend time alone in prayer?

_____

How important is it for me to spend time with others in prayer?

_____

What more do I wish I knew about prayer?

A Prayer List

In making your prayer list, note who you are praying for and what you are praying for. (You may need to get more sheets of paper if you have a lengthy list.)

List as many concerns as you can with as much detail as you can. In this way, many people find that their prayers become more focused.

Name	Petition

Intercessory Prayer List

Are there specific people for whom you feel called to pray regularly? You may not be aware of any particular needs; in a very general way, you may feel led to uphold them in prayer and to petition God for these attributes in their lives:

peace	joy	purpose
health	safety	righteousness
purity	courage	freedom from sin
blessing	hope	increase of faith
discernment	boldness	good fellowship
wisdom	love	good counsel(ors)
faithfulness	mercy	God's grace
prosperity	honor	provision
protection	growth	a sense of direction

List persons for whom you feel led to pray routinely. Also note descriptions you feel are appropriate to their situations or lives.

Name	Petition

Spiritual Battles

Have you ever felt as if you've been through a war spiritually speaking? The more you prayed, the worse things seemed to be—until finally there was a moment of victory and a great sense of relief? Many people refer to this as spiritual warfare.

In Ephesians 6, the apostle Paul noted key elements of armor that a Christian is to wear when engaging in battles against darkness, principalities, and powers in the spiritual realm: girdle of truth, breastplate of righteousness, shoes of preparation of gospel of peace, shield of faith, helmet of salvation, and sword of the Spirit (which is the Word of God).

Do you have a meaning for each of these terms? What do you do personally to put on each of these elements of armor? What practical steps might you take to remind yourself mentally that your mind has been delivered from evil and that you are being renewed mentally as a result of your relationship with Christ Jesus? Note them on the chart on page 22.

As you consider each metaphor, consider the piece of armor that is being described. For example, what is a breastplate? How does it work? And also consider the spiritual term associated with it. What does that spiritual term mean to you? Do you see any connections between the two?

Generally speaking, we engage in spiritual battle related to situations or circumstances that we know to be evil or contrary to God's purposes, but no ready answer or solution for them seems humanly possible. Can you identify any situations or circumstances that fall into that category in your life? Note them in the left column of the chart on page 23.

In every battle situation, there is generally a war objective or an identifiable point at which victory might be declared. Ask yourself, What will I be satisfied

	Meaning of Metaphor to Me	Ways to Achieve or Prepare
Girdle of Truth		
Breastplate of Righteousness		
Shoes of Preparation of Gospel of Peace		
Shield of Faith		
Helmet of Salvation		
Sword of the Spirit (Word of God)		

with? What truly is the will of God that I know He desires to enact in this situation? Note your warfare objective in the middle column.

At times, a battle must be won before a certain date or time. If a date or time frame is associated with victory, note that as part of your objective.

Finally, each battle has a method. The weapons you have at your disposal include fasting (which intensifies prayer), nonstop praying (often including others in a twenty-four-hour prayer chain), asking others to join the battle (involving others in petitioning with one heart and mind), and taking a symbolic action to reinforce purpose in yourself (and others) or to send a signal of your resolve to the enemy. In the right column, note the methodology you believe the Lord is calling you to employ in this battle.

Battlefield	Objective/Point of Victory—Date	Methodology

Serving Others

Service has always been a cornerstone of Christian discipline. We are called to give, and to give freely—even to people for whom we might not feel affection. We are to serve others with generosity, holding nothing back. We are to give service—including money that enables service—willingly, cheerfully, and with faith.

Serving Even Your Enemies

Luke 6:27–28 tells us that we are to love our enemies in three practical ways:

1. "Do good to those who hate you."
2. "Bless those who curse you."
3. "Pray for those who spitefully use you."

In doing good to those who hate us, we are called by God to do good works that will be for their ultimate and eternal good. We are to find ways of building them up, encouraging them, speaking positive words to them, and helping them so that they might come to know the Source of all love.

In blessing others, we are to speak well of them. We are to praise their good deeds and give honor when honor is due. We are to ignore, in essence, their cursing of us and respond with kindness.

In praying for those who use us, we are to ask God to intercede on our behalf, and we are to petition God to meet the deep needs of their lives that compel them to *want* to use or destroy people.

Loving enemies does not mean that we become doormats, however. Love can also be present in confrontation or frank discussion. Abusers are not to be coddled or ignored—but to be helped so that they might not abuse. Abusers are deeply troubled on the inside, and they often have no experiential knowledge of God's love. Saying no to abuse is a possible way of bringing persons to the point where they must deal with their abusive nature and, in the process, have an opportunity to experience God's forgiveness and love in their lives. Prayers, edifying words, and positive deeds that accompany such confrontations often bring hateful persons to repentance and a new life.

On the form, list persons you believe are your enemies. Also note specific ways in which you can extend love to each person.

Enemy	Course of Action

Serving People Who Have Wronged You

One of the greatest acts of service that you can give to people is forgiveness—either to forgive people and free them from the burden of guilt they have been feeling, or to ask their forgiveness and bring about a sense of reconciliation or healing to them.

You may say, "But I am the offended party. Why should I forgive someone who has done me wrong?"

Your forgiving others is essential to your forgiveness. Jesus taught, "Forgive, and you will be forgiven" (Matt. 6:14–15; Luke 6:37).

List persons you need to forgive. Note in the middle column the practical steps you may need to take. Couple your act of forgiveness with a positive thought or feeling about the person; note that in the column to the right.

You may say, "But the person I need to forgive is long gone." The person may be dead, or you may have lost all contact. You still need to find some way to symbolize your forgiveness of that person. One woman wrote a note and stuck it under a rock on a mountain trail; she forgave that person, left all of her resentment and bitterness there, and returned from her hike with a real glow. Another person built a campfire and threw logs on it, each log symbolizing one act of resentment or hurt. Find a way of expressing forgiveness and then doing something positive in that person's memory.

Person I Need to Forgive	Act of Forgiveness I Should Take Toward This Person	Positive Feeling for This Person

Confessing Your Faults

The New Testament admonishes believers to "confess your trespasses to one another, and pray for one another, that you may be healed" (James 5:16).

In admitting faults, weaknesses, and sins, you bring things out in the open so that you might ask forgiveness and consciously make an effort to change your behavior. In confessing your trespasses, you don't always need to confess to the person you have wronged. Sometimes it's better if the person doesn't know what you have done. Still, you need to confess what you know is wrong and what is causing guilt or shame.

Commit your way to the LORD, Trust also in Him, And He shall bring it to pass.
—Psalm 37:5

On the form, you are asked to note what you know you need to confess. If you are uncomfortable writing the exact act of your trespass, write a code word or name that triggers meaning for you alone. Next to that entry, put the name of a person to whom you can confess that wrong—someone who will keep your confession in confidence and pray with you about that sin and the change you seek to make in your life. The result of confessing is healing—of your emotions, psyche, memories, relationships, indeed, your very soul.

Confession to Make	Confessor

Serving Your Family and Neighbors

Sometimes we can get so caught up in serving the needs of nameless and faceless people that we overlook our responsibility to serve people we know and, even more important, loved ones with whom we live. Acts of kindness and courtesy can often alleviate heavy emotional, psychological, or physical burdens.

On the form, you are asked to list your close family and friends and then to identify ways in which you might serve each one better. (Don't overlook people in your church family.) True service bears its own reward. It isn't done with a return favor in mind. Neither does it expect recognition, thanks, or honor. Serving is helping where helping is obviously needed or desired—and often helping without the needy person asking.

Sometimes others don't want your help. Your loving service to them is regarded as an infringement of privacy or as unwanted assistance. Don't assume that your service is unwanted, however. It's too easy to use that stance as a cop-out for getting involved. Ask directly and privately: "Would it be of help to you if I _____?"

"Do it as unto the Lord" is an admonition drawn from Scripture. That's a good position to take in offering service.

Family and Friends I Must Serve	Meaningful Ways of Serving

Keeping God's Commandments

The Bible has hundreds of commandments—some things we are told to do, and other things we are told not to do. Jesus summed up the commandments in a twofold way:

"You shall love the LORD your God with all your heart, with all your soul, and with all your mind." This is the first and great commandment. And the second is like it: "You shall love your neighbor as yourself" (Matt. 22:37–39).

Most of us are familiar with the Ten Commandments (see Ex. 20:2–17), the first portion of the law given to Moses:

1. "You shall have no other gods before Me."
2. "You shall not make for yourself a carved image . . . you shall not bow down to them nor serve them."
3. "You shall not take the name of the LORD your God in vain."
4. "Remember the Sabbath day, to keep it holy."
5. "Honor your father and your mother."
6. "You shall not murder."
7. "You shall not commit adultery."

8. "You shall not steal."
9. "You shall not bear false witness against your neighbor."
10. "You shall not covet . . . anything that is your neighbor's."

First John 2:16 sums up our propensity to sin as being threefold: "the lust of the flesh, the lust of the eyes, and the pride of life." One person restates these three as "I want people," "I want things," and "I want fame and glory."

Many people claim to find it easy to love God, but they have trouble loving other people; others find people easy to deal with but God very difficult to love.

Most of us find ourselves tempted to engage in one of the "you shall not's" more than we find ourselves tempted to engage in other rules on God's list. Reflect on the following questions and make notes about your conclusions:

Do I find it easier to love God or people?

_____

Why do I think that's true in my life?

_____

_____

_____

What might I do to better enhance my ability to love God or perhaps to better express my love to God?

_____

_____

_____

What might I do to better enhance my ability to love others or perhaps to show my love to others?

_____

_____

_____

Do I seem to have a particularly difficult time keeping one of the Ten Commandments?

_____

What more might I do to better resist temptation in that area or to avoid temptation?

_____

_____

_____

What seems to matter more to me: power, money, or fame?

_____

Why do I think that's true in my life?

_____

_____

_____

What might I do to better curb these desires?

_____

_____

How do I relate each of the Ten Commandments to my life today?

_____

_____

_____

_____

_____

_____

_____

_____

_____

_____

_____

_____

_____

_____

_____

Keeping God's Top Ten

Next to each commandment, write a specific way in which you can keep it.

Commandment	Way to Keep This Commandment Today
"You shall have no other gods before Me."	
"You shall not make for yourself a carved image . . . you shall not bow down to them nor serve them."	
"You shall not take the name of the LORD your God in vain."	
"Remember the Sabbath day, to keep it holy."	
"Honor your father and your mother."	
"You shall not murder."	
"You shall not commit adultery."	
"You shall not steal."	
"You shall not bear false witness against your neighbor."	
"You shall not covet . . . anything that is your neighbor's."	

"Lord, Have Mercy!"

In reflecting on your ability to keep God's commandments, you probably reached the conclusion that has been echoed through the centuries: "Lord, have mercy on me!"

There isn't a great deal you can do to plan away temptation to sin. But you can recognize your propensity to sin and the ways in which you are easily tempted. You can plan your life in such a way to avoid areas of temptation.

Don't be discouraged by facing the hard reality that may be your present spiritual nature. The Lord's promise to us is that when we turn to Him and confess our sins, "He is faithful and just to forgive us our sins, and to cleanse us from all unrighteousness" (1 John 1:9). The Lord's desire for you is a renewal of every aspect of your life until you become like His Son, Jesus Christ—a person fully alive with the power of the Holy Spirit. God's desire is that you be fully who He created you to be, with all of your best traits and abilities and talents in full operation, free of sin, and in loving and joyful relationship with others.

Each time you recognize that you have fallen short of that goal, you can turn to the heavenly Father and say, "I realize this isn't what You desire for me. It isn't Your best. It isn't what will truly make me happy, fulfilled, or at peace. Help me to conform my will to Your will. Please renew my thinking and help me to plan my life—and then live out my life—in a way that is pleasing to You."

The good news of the gospel is that when you do this with a sincere, genuine desire, the Lord will do what you ask! He will help you repent—or change your mind, will, and direction—and follow after Him. He will give you the courage to confront your enemies without and your enemies within. He will change you and strengthen you and make you ever more whole.

My Plea for God's Mercy

Write out your prayer of hope and desire for the Lord's will in your life.

_____

_____

_____

_____

■ Summing Up and Setting Goals

The greatest experience of your entire existence will be the moment that you finally see Jesus Christ face-to-face. In that moment, priorities will become very clear.

You will see goals for what they truly are. Motivations will be revealed—even those of which you may not be aware. You will truly be "known" even as you "know."

The good news is that you have an opportunity to envision that moment this side of eternity and adjust your life in preparation for that great eye-to-eye, heart-to-heart encounter with the Lord.

As you look back over the pages in this chapter, identify the things that seem to be repeated in your notes.

Look especially for

- ways in which you want to grow spiritually.
- ways in which you seek to employ your spiritual gifts.
- the nourishment you desire to give to your spirit.
- those for whom you want to pray and have a desire to serve.
- changes you believe you should make in your behavior, desires, or attitudes.

Summary Statements

Write in one paragraph or less your heart's desire toward the things of God.

_____

_____

_____

_____

Write in one paragraph or less the changes that you need to make in your spiritual discipline in order to become the person you truly want to be. State these changes in a positive way, not as a condemnation or an expression of guilt.

_____

_____

_____

_____

Write in one paragraph or less the reason that you seek to grow spiritually. What do you believe will be the result of such growth?

_____

_____

_____

_____

Note any major recurring words, phrases, themes, or ideas as you have described your spiritual nature or relationships. Do they convey any message to you?

_____

_____

_____

_____

Identify in a few words how you feel when you think about the Lord or about spiritual things.

_____

_____

_____

If you had to write just one word or phrase to motivate yourself toward or remind yourself of the need of greater spiritual growth, what would that word or phrase be?

_____

Goal Statements

As you reflect on this chapter and the summary statements you have written, frame goals related to your spiritual growth. Goal statements are action steps you truly intend to take. (You'll find guidelines in the featured segment "Writing Good Goal Statements.")

Examples of spiritual goal statements are given below:

Ineffective:
Develop a better prayer life.
Be more disciplined in my Bible reading.

Effective:
I will spend at least ten minutes a day alone with the Lord as a time to speak to Him and hear His voice in my heart.
I will read at least two chapters of the Bible each day.

Your goals can be short-range, mid-range, and long-range. They can be linked to others in regard to service or affiliation, but your spiritual growth goals should be singularly your own.

Writing Good Goal Statements

    1. Always use personal pronouns. Words such as "I," "my," "mine," and "me" will personalize your statements and make them easier to affirm and assimilate.
Ineffective: "Jogging is good exercise."
Effective: "I enjoy jogging three miles every day."

    2. Keep your statements in the present tense. Referring to the past or future dilutes the impact of, or may be counterproductive to, the internalization of your goals.
Ineffective: "Someday I'll go to Hawaii."
Effective: "I love the surf and sand in Maui."

    3. Keep your goal statements short and concise (only four to five seconds long when spoken aloud).
Ineffective: "Now that I have saved five thousand dollars, I may go into business for myself and I hope to succeed."
Effective: "My business is properly capitalized with the five thousand dollars I put in it."

    4. Direct your goals toward what you desire, instead of toward goals that focus on a negative behavior you want to stop. Your mind can't concentrate on the reverse of an idea. If you try to tell yourself not to repeat mistakes, your mind will reinforce the mistake. You want to focus your current dominant thought on your desires, not your dislikes.
Ineffective: "I can quit smoking."
              "I will lose twenty pounds."
              "I am not late any more."
              "I don't yell at the children."
              "I won't fumble the football."
Effective: "I am in control of my habits."
              "I weigh a slim, trim _____ pounds."
              "I arrive early for appointments."
              "I am patient and loving with my kids."
              "I guard and control the football."

    5. Keep your goals noncompetitive, rather than comparing yourself with others.
Ineffective: "I will become a starter on the team before he or she does."
Effective: "I am starting on the team and doing the job well."

    6. In writing your goal statements, strive for improvement over your current status. Don't strive for perfection.
Ineffective: "I'm the best sales executive in the company, making the most money."
Effective: "I'm doing my best this year, producing twenty percent more than last year."

—Seeds of Greatness

My Spiritual Growth Goals

Write your goals related to your spiritual development.

_____

_____

_____

_____

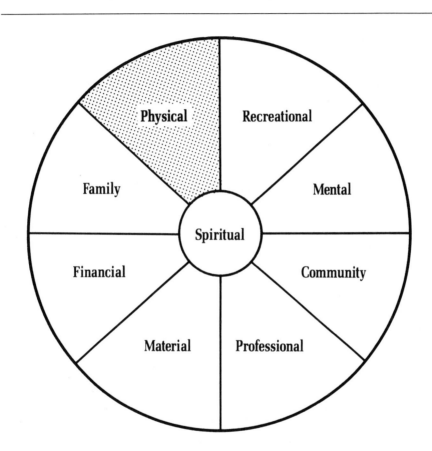

SECRET: Your body is a temple and should be treated as such.

SCRIPTURE: "But those who wait on the LORD
        Shall renew their strength;
        They shall mount up with wings like eagles,
        They shall run and not be weary,
        They shall walk and not faint" (Isa. 40:31).

2

Anticipating
Better Health

NINE TIMES out of ten when I visit a physician or health specialist, the first question asked is this: "Well, what seems to be the problem today?"

Recently, I surprised a physician by responding, "No problem. I'm in good health. I feel great. I thought it might be helpful for me to visit you on a day like today so we can discuss how I can *stay* feeling like this and perhaps even feel better."

He was stunned, and for a moment, he didn't say anything. Finally, he said, "Denis, I've never had a patient say to me what you just said. And I can't tell you how much I wish every one of my patients would take time to come to me *before* they get sick. I could spare most of them a lot of discomfort and pain."

"But don't your patients come to you for annual physicals?" I asked.

"That was much more common ten years ago than it is today," he said. "I'm not sure exactly when things changed, but you'd be surprised how many people *don't* have an annual physical exam now—even though most of my patients would probably agree that having an annual physical is an excellent idea."

Why don't people have physicals? I've talked with a number of physicians and patients about this and the reasons seem clustered into these categories:

- "I don't have the time."
- "I don't want to spend the money on a lot of tests."
- "I can't afford to miss work."
- "I'm feeling fine, so why go?"
- "It's not covered by my insurance policy."
- "I just haven't thought about it. I guess maybe a year *has* gone by."

DREAM A LITTLE DREAM:
Completing the Biggest Race of Your Life—
Exhausted but Joyful

Take a few minutes to imagine that you have just completed the race of your life. All communication systems were destroyed in your town, and you were entrusted by your community to run to a neighboring town under the cloak of darkness with news of impending danger. Your community knows that if you arrive in time, the neighboring town can take measures to save itself. Now, you have completed your journey, just as the sun is rising. Even though you were in excellent shape, you have run faster than you ever thought you could run. The message has been delivered. Your mission has been accomplished. Although you are exhausted, you feel vital, healthy, and fully alive as your friends in the town pour refreshing jugs of water over you. Already, steps are being taken to save both your town and the town in which you have arrived.

Think about your body. How does it feel in this moment? What kinds of energy do you feel? How much do you weigh? What is the fitness level of your body? What is the texture of your skin? What do you desire to do as you cool down and begin to relax? What would you like to eat after such an exhilarating experience? What kind of garment do you desire to put on?

Write freely as thoughts and images come to your mind:

_____

_____

_____

_____

_____

_____

_____

_____

_____

_____

_____

_____

_____

_____

All of these are understandable reasons—but not good ones. In planning for better health, plan on an annual physical.

Your physical inventory is vital to visualizing a physical level of well-being that is personalized, progressive (both incremental and gradual), and practical. Those goals, in turn, will give you the framework for developing a plan that is set in time—with daily, weekly, seasonal, and annual things to do. The results? Improved health and well-being for nearly every person!

Begin by conducting a personal and comprehensive physical inventory.

■ Your Physical Inventory

This inventory has three main facets to it:

1. *A physical history.* Physicians begin at this point, and so should you. A physical history will give you a clear overview of your health—general weaknesses and strengths, and immediate needs. The inventory provided here goes beyond a basic medical form to include several other evaluative approaches.
2. *Health attitudes.* How do you feel about your body? Your appearance? Your health habits? The importance of physical recreation and relaxation? This part of the inventory focuses on your attitudes, opinions, and ideas related to health.
3. *Health patterns.* An inventory of health patterns gives an overview of what you do on a daily, weekly, monthly, and yearly basis to improve or maintain your health (or fail to maintain your health).

The three aspects of the health inventory are interrelated, of course. At the conclusion of the inventory, you'll find a series of questions for helping you make these connections and begin to make a plan to act on your conclusions.

■ A Physical History

You may want to complete these pages and then photocopy them to place in a general family medical file for quick reference when it is time to have an annual physical or to complete insurance applications. You may want to have a form for each family member to complete.

If you are going to improve your health, moving from one level of health upward to the next, you must first isolate your current problems and be very objective about your current level of health. A basic physical history is the place to begin.

Basic Physical History

Be honest with yourself. These forms need never be seen by anyone other than you unless you want to share the information. You list these facts so that you can set goals and map a plan for *improved* health.

I am the Lord who heals you. —Exodus 15:2(

Date of birth: _____   Weight: _____

Height: _____   Heart rate: _____

Blood pressure: _____

Known or suspected allergies (including adverse reactions to any medications):

_____

_____

_____

_____

_____

_____

_____

_____

Hospitalizations (including day surgeries):

Reason	Hospital	Date	Attending Physician

X-rays or other major medical tests and their results:

Test	Facility in Which Test Conducted	Date	Results	Contact Physician

Recurring or chronic health problems:

_____

_____

_____

_____

_____

_____

_____

_____

Major injuries (include broken bones, sprains, back injuries, wounds, concussions—be sure to note any complications):

Type of Injury; Area of Body Affected	Year

Medications presently taken regularly (including vitamin and mineral supplements):

Name	Dosage	Frequency

Immunizations:

Type	Month and Year

For men:

Do you conduct regular self-examination for prostate cancer? _____

Most recent urological exam: _____

For women:

Date of onset of menstruation: _____

Are periods regular? _____

Is flow moderate to light? _____

Do you conduct regular self-examination of breasts? _____

Children (give date of birth for each child; list any miscarriages or stillborn births):

_____

_____

_____

_____

Most recent mammogram: _____

Most recent gynecological exam: _____

Medical Visits Record

Many people roam from physician to physician, or fail to have their medical records transferred when they move. The result is an incomplete record and missing information that may be vital to treatment in emergencies. If you are unable to construct a record of visits in the distant past, attempt to construct a record for the last year. (You may be able to reconstruct this from your check register or insurance records.) And then get in the habit of recording each visit to a health specialist.

From time to time, review your medical visits record. Are you going to health specialists more frequently? Are you experiencing a recurrence of an ailment?

List visits to all physicians, including dentists, eye doctors, and other specialists. (Use this form to get started. You may need to use more sheets.)

Date	Physician Visited	Reason	Diagnosis/Treatment

Environmental History

Scientists are discovering more and more linkages between the level of health we enjoy and the environments in which we live. Here's a very basic environmental history that a physician or an allergist may find helpful in isolating and treating a medical problem you may have.

One woman who did this history felt quite good about the city, neighborhood, and home in which she lived. But she realized that since she had been transferred to an open-room work environment, with shared telephones, computer keyboards, and fairly close proximity to other workers, her incidences of colds and flu had increased dramatically.

In yet another case, a man realized with new insight that the air circulation in his place of business probably was not adequate since frequent chemical odors invaded the work area and there were times when his coworkers complained of headaches or a feeling of stuffiness in the office. Building engineers ultimately verified a problem, and several modifications were made to the building that resulted in improved breathing and fewer headaches for all the workers.

Environmental Residency History

Note the places you have lived, and rate the quality of those environments.

Residences/ Years	Environmental Features	Water Quality	Air Quality	Other

As you reflect on your current environment, make notes about each of the following:

Air quality (adequate ventilation; humidity; smokers in residence; drafts; adequate heat or cooling):

_____

_____

_____

Water quality (bottled water; chemical taste; discoloration):

_____

_____

Areas that may produce mold or fungal growth or cause proliferation of allergens or dust mites (leaking pipes; dusty or littered areas):

_____

_____

General appraisal:

_____

_____

Review of Work Environment

Evaluate the environment in which you work.

Air quality (adequate ventilation; humidity; smokers; drafts; adequate heat or cooling):

_____

_____

Water quality (cleanliness of water coolers; chemical taste to water; discoloration):

_____

_____

Vending machines and food preparation areas (clean; well serviced; adequate refrigeration or high enough cooking heat):

_____

_____

Areas that may produce mold or fungal growth or cause proliferation of allergens or dust mites (leaking pipes; dusty or littered areas):

_____

_____

Shared equipment or facilities (clean, personalized or communal use of receivers; adequate space):

_____

_____

Enforced sick-employee policy:

_____

_____

What are the procedures in place to protect against equipment or chemical misuse?

_____

_____

What other businesses or manufacturing operations are within close range of your workplace? Do you know what they manufacture or what chemicals and processes may be in use?

_____

_____

A Family Health History

Are you a member of a family that seems to have a history of death from a particular ailment, such as breast cancer or stroke? Do you seem to take after one parent or member of your family in your basic health profile? Avail yourself of current testing and procedures to alleviate or diagnose certain family-related health problems.

Did you grow up in a house where all the adults smoked virtually nonstop or were alcoholics? Was your childhood diet healthy and balanced?

Find out as much as you can about your parents' and grandparents' health histories. The information may be very useful to you, to your children, or to your community.

Family Health Tree

Cite age of death, cause of death, and general health conditions for each person you can in your family tree.

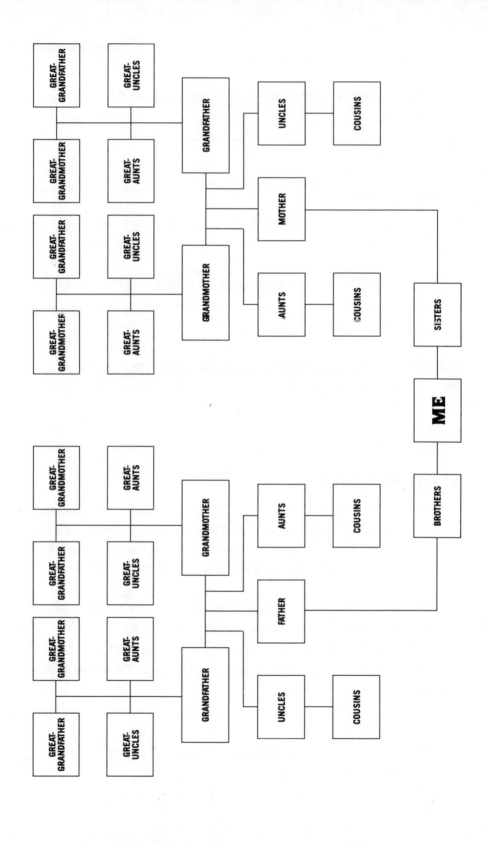

Family Health Patterns

Answer the following questions regarding the general health of your parents and other relatives:

How would you describe the general health of persons in your immediate family when you were a child?

_____

_____

What types of ailments did your parents tend to have at your age?

_____

_____

Were any of your family members chronically ill or ill for a long period of time?

_____

_____

How would you describe your general diet as a

    young child?

_____

_____

    teenager?

_____

_____

    young adult?

_____

_____

How would you describe the general activity level of your family members when you were a child?

_____

_____

What has been your general activity level in the past?

_____

_____

Is there any history of chemical use in your family (tobacco, alcohol, prescription drugs, other drugs)?

_____

_____

Is there a history of psychological disorders in your family?

_____

_____

What types of medications did your mother take when she was pregnant with you?

_____

_____

Is there any history of problems with any medications during pregnancy in your family?

_____

_____

Have any family members had birth defects? If yes, are they genetically linked?

_____

_____

Are there any genetically linked disorders in your family tree?

_____

_____

What types of medications did your grandmothers take during pregnancy with your parents?

_____

_____

How would you describe the prevailing attitude of your family (when you were a child) toward

physical health?

_____

_____

mental health?

_____

_____

physicians?

_____

_____

dentists?

_____

_____

health specialists?

_____

_____

hospitals?

_____

_____

surgery?

_____

_____

medications?

_____

_____

vitamins and minerals?

_____

_____

basic hygiene and health practices?

_____

_____

What is the prevailing attitude of your closest friends toward sickness and health?

_____

_____

_____

_____

Researching your family's health history may be a sobering experience. Don't be discouraged. This is one case in which what you don't know might hurt you. In many cases, you can make adjustments or reverse long-standing trends or habits. In other cases, you can discuss your family health patterns with a physician and avail yourself of early warning sign tests and treatments.

■ Your Attitudes and Opinions About Your Physical Well-Being

In this section, you'll find a number of questions related to the way you think and feel about health-related issues. Again, be honest with yourself.

Your attitudes about health, exercise, diet, and general physical well-being are critical when it comes to developing a personal health-improvement plan that you will stick with. Just about anybody can define a good health program. Eat lots of fresh fruits and vegetables, exercise regularly, avoid chemicals that are bad for you, and avoid eating too much fat and sugar. Knowing what to do isn't nearly as important as *believing* that your health can improve and *valuing* improved health. How you feel about your health will keep you exercising, eating right, and getting all of the medical help available to you.

Exploring Your Basic Health Attitudes

1. Am I a physically healthy person?

   On a scale of 1 to 10 (with 10 being perfect health), how would you rate your level of health today? _____

What do you believe your state of health will be a year from now

if you implement a health-improvement plan? _____

if you don't implement such a plan? _____

Do you think of yourself as being a healthy person with periodic bouts of sickness, or a sick person who struggles to have periods of good health?

I am a _____ person who _____

_____ .

2. What do I believe stands in my way of becoming a healthier person?

Check all items that you believe apply to your life, and list any others that come to mind:

☐ Insufficient information

What do you need to know more about? _____
Where can you get that information? _____

☐ Friends or family members unconcerned about health

Do you know anyone who is concerned about health? _____
Might you convince your friends to be more concerned? _____

☐ Bad habits

Which habits do you believe are bad? _____

☐ Chemical addiction

Name any chemicals you habitually use (include all of your medications and such items as caffeine, alcohol, and tobacco). Put a check mark beside any that you believe contribute to your being less healthy than you might be if you didn't use that substance.

_____   _____   _____

_____   _____   _____

_____   _____   _____

3. How much time (during a day) do I believe it takes for me to maintain physical health?

How do you believe that time is to be broken down (for example, among exercise, eating, sleeping)? _____

_____

Do you not know that those who run in a race all run, but one receives the prize? Run in such a way that you may obtain it. And everyone who competes for the prize is temperate in all things. Now they do it to obtain a perishable crown, but we for an imperishable crown. Therefore I run thus: not with uncertainty. Thus I fight: not as one who beats the air. But I discipline my body and bring it into subjection, lest, when I have preached to others, I myself should become disqualified.
—1 Corinthians 9:24–27

Do you spend that much time in a day in activities directly related to your health? _____

4. What reason(s) do I have for wanting to improve my health?

_____

_____

_____

5. Who besides me would benefit from my having improved health?

_____

_____

6. What do I believe would be an ideal schedule for a healthful day?

_____

_____

_____

7. How do I feel about my body?

Do you like the way your body looks (generally speaking)? _____

Do you like the way your body feels (most of the time)? _____

How do you feel about your present weight? _____

How do you feel about your current level of activity? _____

Is there one area (or more) of your body that you don't like? _____

8. Why do I believe I find it difficult to maintain healthy habits or a regimen aimed at improved health (if I do find it difficult)?

_____

_____

_____

9. What do I believe to be the links between mental and emotional health and physical health?

_____

_____

_____

10. What do I believe are benefits I gain from being sick?

Do you have less responsibility when you are sick? _____

Do you get more attention when you are sick? _____

Do you feel you have an excuse when you are sick? _____

11. How long do I believe I am going to live?

On what is this belief based? _____

Do you believe it's possible to change your life expectancy? _____

What might you do to change your estimated year of death? _____

Is this how long you *want* to live? _____

12. Who can I really count on to support or applaud an improvement in my health?

Are you capable of applauding your success without an audience to applaud you? _____

What kinds of rewards (include tangible and intangible ones) do you expect from being in better health?

_____

_____

Who will give those rewards? _____

13. How do I feel about exercise?

Do you like to exercise? _____

Do you like to exercise alone or with others? _____

Do you feel you must sweat in order to improve? _____

Do you believe that without pain, there's no gain? _____

Do you believe that some exercises are better for you than others? _____

Which ones? _____

Why? _____

_____

14. Do I believe that my appearance (including my weight) is related to my self-worth?

Is exercise related to your self-esteem? _____

Is your health level a part of your reputation? _____

15. How much importance do I believe other people place on my health and physical appearance?

Who are they? _____

Is their opinion important to you? _____

Why? _____

_____

16. Do I believe that my overall level of physical health is related to my spiritual health? _____

In what ways? _____

_____

17. In what ways do I believe my physical health is related to my job performance?

_____

_____

18. In what ways do I believe my physical health is related to my ability to create?

_____

_____

19. In what ways does my level of physical well-being affect my social relationships? _____

_____

20. What is more important to me than my health? _____

_____

Do you sacrifice your health for those things? _____

21. How have my attitudes and opinions about health changed over the last ten years?

Was there ever a time when you were more concerned about your level of health than you are now? _____

Why do you think these changes have occurred? _____

_____

■ Your Health Habits

In this section, you will be giving yourself information that will enable you (or a health specialist) to take a look at the broad trends and habits of your life.

Consumption and Use Patterns

Identify your health habits related to each of these categories.

Tobacco

Do you smoke? _____
When did you start smoking? _____
How many years have you smoked? _____
What do you presently smoke? _____
How much in a day? _____
Have you increased the amount you smoke in the last year? _____
What changes have you noticed in your life
     since you started smoking? _____
     since you increased your smoking? _____

Alcohol

Do you drink alcohol? _____
How much do you consume in a day? _____
How much in a week? _____
Is this more or less than you consumed this time last year? _____
Have you noticed any changes in your life since this change in your consumption? _____

Chemicals

Do you use any drugs on a regular or periodic basis? _____
     What? _____
     How often? _____

Do you suspect that you may be addicted to a chemical? _____
     What? _____
     Why? _____

Medications

Have you started taking any new medications in the last year? _____
     What? _____
     Why? _____

Have you increased the dosage or frequency of any of your medications in the last
year? _____
     What? _____
     Why? _____
     To what level of frequency? _____
     Does your physician know of this change in dosage or frequency? _____

Have you noticed any changes in your life since you began or increased a medication? _____

Have you experienced any side effects from medications? _____
     What? _____
     From which ones? _____

If you are a married female of child-bearing age, are you using a form of artificial
birth control? _____
     What? _____
     Since when? _____
     Have you experienced any of the side effects noted on the packaging inserts?
     _____

How many rounds of antibiotics have you taken in the last year? _____
     _____
     Was this a usual year? _____
     Did you have times in your life in which you took a great many antibiotics?
     _____

Do you habitually suffer from any of these ailments?

- ☐ Bladder infections
- ☐ Rectal bleeding
- ☐ Sharp pains
- ☐ Dull pain
- ☐ Sinus drainage
- ☐ Yeast infections
- ☐ Urinary tract infections
- ☐ Prostate problems

You Have Control!

Although there are many things in life over which you have no control, there are at least twelve things over which you have vast or sole control:

1. YOU can control what you do with most of your time in a day.
2. YOU can control the amount of energy you exert or the amount of effort you give to a task.
3. YOU can control what you think about—your thoughts and imaginations.
4. YOU can control your attitude.
5. YOU can control your tongue. You can choose to remain silent or choose to speak. If you choose to speak, you can choose the words you will say. As you speak the words, you can choose the tone of voice you will use.
6. YOU can control with whom you will develop friendships . . . whom you will choose as role models . . . and whom you will seek out for mentoring counsel and inspiration. You can control to a great extent with whom you will communicate.
7. YOU can control your commitments.
8. YOU can control the causes to which you give your time and ideas.
9. YOU can control your memberships.
10. YOU can control what you do with your faith.
11. YOU can control your concerns—and whether you will choose action or worry in response to them.
12. YOU can control your response to difficult times and people.

—Timing Is Everything

Food

How would you rate your current diet?

	Too Little	About Right	Too Much
Protein			
Carbohydrates			
Fresh fruits			
Fresh vegetables			
Dairy products			
Sugary foods			
Fat			
Caffeine			
Fiber			
Salt			
Water			
Junk foods			

What food items do you think you should eliminate or reduce the amount you consume? _____

What food items do you think you should add or increase in your diet?

_____

Do you regularly eat breakfast? _____

Do you allow yourself to become overly famished before eating? _____

Do you eat even when you aren't hungry? _____

Do you ever force yourself to vomit after eating? _____

Do you take laxatives regularly? _____

Do you take antacid or stomach-calming aids regularly? _____

Do you overeat at any one meal? _____

Do you have frequent cravings for certain types of foods? _____

When you find yourself craving food, what do you do? _____

Do you space out your meals fairly evenly during a day? _____

Do you have a habit of eating a big meal and then going to sleep? _____

Do you snack often? _____

Vitamins and Minerals

Do you regularly take vitamin or mineral supplements? _____

Name them: _____

_____

For how long have you followed this regimen? _____

Have you noticed any change in the way you feel since you began this regimen? _____

Exercise

How do you rate your current level of exercise?

	Too Little	About Right	Too Much
Cardiovascular exercise (aerobic exercise; running; swimming; walking)			
Stretching exercises			
Muscle-building exercises (including isometric and strength-building exercises)			

What do you think you should do to improve your physical exercise level? _____

_____

Have you had any periodic or chronic ailments resulting from exercise? _____

_____

If you have, identify them. _____

_____

From past experience, where in your body do you feel you are especially prone to injury? _____

Sleep and Rest

How much sleep do you currently get in a twenty-four-hour period? _____
    Is your sleep uninterrupted? _____
    Do you awaken feeling rested? _____
    Do you dream extensively? _____
    If you awaken, do you have difficulty returning to sleep? _____
    Do you have a different sleep pattern on weekends from that of weekdays?
    _____

What do you do to relax and unwind?
    What types of activities? _____
    How often? _____
    Do they truly help you relax and unwind? _____
    Do you play games or engage in sporting activities with a highly competitive attitude? _____

How would you evaluate your current level of stress (low, moderate, or high)?
_____
    Has this level of stress changed in the last six months? _____
    What happens to you when stress increases? (Note physical signs as well as habits.) _____
    When did you last experience a day that you felt was truly restful? _____
    When did you last take off a long weekend? _____
    When did you last take a vacation (of a week or longer)? _____

■ Personal Appearance

For the most part, we have concentrated on your physical health and fitness. Your physical appearance is also important to you, for both psychological and social reasons. Answer these nine questions about your appearance:

1. How important are looks to me? _____

2. Do I like my appearance? _____

   If not, what would you change?

   _____

   What might be involved in making these changes?

   _____

3. Do I wear clothing and accessories to enhance or detract from my physical body shape and attributes? _____

   If you wear clothing to detract, why? _____

   _____

4. What is my body type?

   Describe your body by shape or other descriptive terms.

   _____

   Do you choose clothing appropriate for your body type? _____

   Do you know what types of clothing best enhance your body type? _____

   If not, do you know how to get this information? _____

5. What is the condition of my skin?

   Describe the texture and nature of your skin. _____

   _____

   What do you do to maintain healthy skin? _____

   _____

   Do you engage in any habits that can cause potential damage to your skin (such as excessive tanning)? _____

   What more might you do to improve your skin texture? _____

   _____

Are there skin aberrations that you need to have checked, such as irregular or rapidly growing moles? _____

Are there skin aberrations you would like to have removed, such as warts, moles, or birthmarks? _____

6. What is the condition of my hair?

   Describe its texture, condition, and general nature. _____
   _____

   Are you satisfied with your current hairstyle? _____

   If not, what steps might you take to make a change? _____
   _____

7. What is the condition of my nails?

   Describe their appearance and texture. _____
   _____

   Are you satisfied with your nail care? _____

   If not, what changes might you make? _____
   _____

8. What is the condition of my teeth?

   Describe their condition. _____

   Is there something you would like to change about them? _____

9. What other outward changes would I like to make in my general appearance?
   _____

   If you have listed major cosmetic changes, such as ones that require a complete makeover or surgery, ask yourself why this is important to you. What do you hope to gain as the result of such a drastic measure? _____
   _____
   _____

■ Summing Up and Setting Goals

In many ways, you can't set goals related to other areas of your life beyond your ability to live out those goals in your physical body. The good news is that no matter what shape and level of health you are in today, you can probably improve your health through more diligent care.

As you reflect on this chapter, identify things that you readily know to be red flags. In particular, note

- habits that you know are the cause of poor health (now or in the future).
- trends that you'd like to see reversed.
- health habits over which you have control.

Summary Statements

Write in one paragraph or less your greatest concern about your health.

_____

_____

_____

_____

_____

Write in one paragraph or less what gives you the greatest hope about your health.

_____

_____

_____

_____

_____

Reflect on the reference to Jesus as the Great Physician. To what extent and in what ways do you believe the Lord is concerned about and involved in your physical health and well-being?

_____

_____

_____

_____

_____

Note any major recurring theme or thought that you have in response to this chapter. If you had just one word or phrase to motivate yourself toward or remind yourself of the need for greater physical health, what would that word or phrase be?

_____

_____

_____

Goal Statements

As you reflect on your statements and your responses in this chapter, begin to form goal statements for yourself that reflect your true intentions about your health habits and level of fitness. What do you intend to do to improve your physical well-being?

Examples of vague and specific physical health goal statements are given below.

Ineffective:
Exercise more.
Diet.

Effective:
I will do aerobic exercise twenty minutes a day, three times a week.
I will weigh _____ pounds by _____(*date*).

Your goals related to your health can be short-range, mid-range, or long-range. They should be goals that do not depend on the cooperation or participation of another person.

My Health-Related Physical Goals

Write your goals for improving your physical well-being.

_____

_____

_____

_____

_____

_____

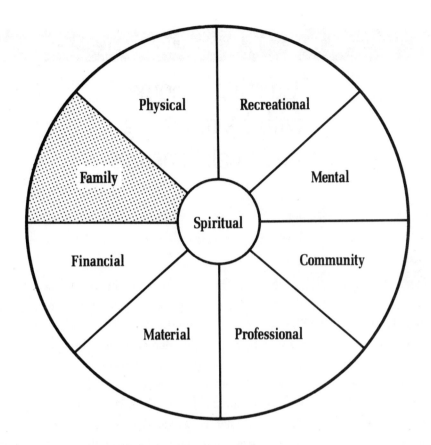

SECRET: To have a happy family is to enjoy an earlier heaven.

SCRIPTURES: "Train up a child in the way he should go, and when he is old he will not depart from it" (Prov. 22:6).

"Nevertheless, neither is man independent of woman, nor woman independent of man, in the Lord" (1 Cor. 11:11).

THE SECRET OF

Creating a Home
with More Loving
Family Relationships

O NE OUTGROWTH of the restructuring of the family in the last few decades has been a concern that new family relationships be bolstered in as many ways as possible. When the traditional family structure was regarded as the norm in our society, we saw few books or articles being written about how to be a father or what to do to help latchkey children. Single parenting, though not unknown three or four decades ago, was much less common. Generally speaking, far fewer women were in the full-time workforce outside the home. Much less planning related to the family needed to be done. That's not the case at all in today's world.

In planning for a balanced, whole life, you must give family an equal billing with all other plans that you make. Don't assume that family will just happen. Creating a high-morale, high-love, high-commitment-to-one-another family takes time, effort, and forethought.

If you are a single person, this chapter is also for you. You are still a member of a family, even if you don't live in a close family relationship with others. If you desire to be married or are about to be married, this is an especially important chapter for you as you appraise how you want your family to function.

■ Defining the Family Unit

A family unit can be defined in several ways—by relationships, by history, by traits and abilities. In thinking about your family, don't limit yourself to traditional charts and roles.

DREAM A LITTLE DREAM:
Sitting Down to the Most Fabulous Family Feast

Take a few minutes to imagine that you have been issued an invitation to the most lavish banquet ever given. All of your loved ones will be present, and all of them will love you as they never have before. The communication flows freely as you sit down at the table spread before you. You are waited on with the most tender expressions of care. There's music in the air, mingling with aromas from your favorite dishes and the perfumes worn by your beloved family members.

Savor this moment. What do you desire to share with your family members? What are they saying to you? How would you describe your relationship with each one? What sounds capture your attention? What sights inspire you? What are they looking for you to do and say to them? What do you anticipate doing together as you leave the table, full of energy and nourished as you never have been before?

Write freely as thoughts and images come to your mind:

_____
_____
_____
_____
_____
_____
_____
_____
_____
_____
_____
_____
_____
_____
_____
_____
_____
_____
_____
_____
_____
_____
_____

Family Members and Their Traits

Who do you consider to be in your family? A family member might be a godparent, a close friend who is known to your children as an aunt or uncle, or a foster child who is temporarily a part of your home.

We are members
of one another.
—Ephesians 4:25

On separate sheets of paper, list all of your family members by name and relationship. Then highlight (or underline) the ones you consider to be part of your immediate family. Put an asterisk next to the ones you see daily or weekly.

Now create a new list of the persons whom you see daily or weekly and whom you consider to be a part of your immediate family. Beside each name, note several traits about that person and the person's function in your family (for example, earns half of family money, takes care of children, keeps house clean and functioning, brings most of the news of the outside world into the family, is chief idea originator).

Reflecting on Family Roles

As you reflect on the members of your family and their basic functional roles within your family, ask yourself these questions. (You may want to use the questions as thought starters and expand your answers.)

Are there members of my family that I wish I saw more often, or that I wish played a more integral role in the functioning of my family?

_____

_____

_____

Are there some functions that seem misplaced or that I would like to see transferred to another person?

_____

_____

_____

Is someone filling a function or taking a role that I believe is rightfully mine?

_____

_____

_____

If so, what might I do to regain that role or take over the responsibility for that function?

_____

_____

_____

Is there someone in my family I shun? Why? Are my reasons truly justifiable? What do I lose by not associating with that person? Is it possible for the relationship to be reestablished or healed?

_____

_____

_____

Family Gift Giving

Use index cards or a section of a record book to list each close family member. Then identify three or more gifts that you know this person would like to receive (within the next two to three years). You may want to note a special occasion when giving such a gift would be most appropriate, such as a graduation or milestone birthday or anniversary.

Your Family History

Briefly tell your family history. You may type it up, write it out, or even tape-record it.

■ The Family Atmosphere

One way to look at a family is to describe the family atmosphere—the tenor of the relationships, the way the family feels to its own members, the bonds shared by the family.

Family Time and Space

Answer the following questions:

Does each member of your family have a space (room or portion of a room) to call his or her own? _____

Does each member of your family have a time when he or she can be alone in your home (or in his or her room)? _____

Do you require your children to participate in family activities (even if they don't initially want to participate)? _____

Do you require yourself to participate in family activities (even if you don't particularly want to participate)? _____

How many hours of a typical week do family members spend together? (Only count the time when all family members are present and awake.) _____

When you are all together as a family, what activities are you likely to be doing? List them:

_____

_____

_____

_____

_____

_____

_____

Do not provoke your children to wrath, but bring them up in the training and admonition of the Lord.
—Ephesians 6:4

Place an asterisk next to the activities that provide for communication among family members. Time spent watching TV together doesn't count unless you actively discuss the programs. Eating dinner together may be a shared activity, but it may not provide for active communication. Driving twenty miles to church may be something you hadn't thought of as a family activity, but it is something you do together as a family that may very well provide a time for active communication.

Now put a plus sign next to activities that provide an opportunity for you to touch one another (hug, pat on the back, hold hands, and so forth). As you watch television, you may sit close to a child or spouse, even if you aren't talking.

Relational Family History

List three of the times that you believe your family members would agree were family highlights—fun or meaningful times spent together:

1. _____
2. _____
3. _____

What is the most meaningful time you have ever spent with your family?

_____

_____

Pause to reflect quietly for a few minutes. Let your imagination wander. What would you like to experience with your family—to see with them, to talk with them about, to share with them, to enjoy together—that you haven't yet experienced? Identify one or more specific experiences:

_____

_____

Family Communication

If you are single, adapt this section to relate to the communication you presently have with members of your initial childhood family and with friends. If you are dating someone seriously or are engaged to be married, consider that person to be your family in this exercise.

When you communicate as a family, what topics do you generally talk about?

_____

_____

_____

What do you tend to fight about or argue about in your family?

_____

_____

_____

When was the last time you all enjoyed a belly laugh together? What was the joke, circumstance, or story that had you all laughing?

_____

_____

_____

Where would you place your family communication on these continuums?

| Mostly humorous | —————┼————— | Mostly serious |

| Mostly affirmative of one another | —————┼————— | Mostly critical of one another |

| Long, involved discussions and conversations | —————┼————— | Matter-of-fact statements |

| Marked by genuine concern and love | —————┼————— | Marked by anger, bitterness, hostility, or resentment |

| Plenty of time for questions and complete answers | —————┼————— | Never enough time for full answers to questions |

| Room for disagreement and exchange of differing opinions | —————┼————— | Dictatorial or domineering style demanding agreement |

| Easy flowing | —————┼————— | Stilted |

| Uninterrupted | —————┼————— | Hurried |

| Innocent and playful teasing | —————┼————— | Harsh and hurtful teasing |

| No off-limits subjects | —————┼————— | Lots of taboo issues or subjects |

Using six adjectives or less, how would you summarize the nature of the general communication in your home? _____

Are you satisfied with this definition of your family communication? _____

If not, what might you do to bring about change in it? _____
_____
_____

Has your overall family communication changed significantly in recent days, weeks, months, or years? If so, can you identify what may have caused that change? (The change may have been as dramatic as a divorce, as innocent as one child moving away to college, or as troublesome as a child's beginning to use drugs.)
_____
_____

Have you dealt fully with that issue that caused the change in communication? _____

What are some ways by which you might compensate for the change or bring about better communication in spite of the change? _____
_____
_____
_____

Evaluating Your Family Life

Reflect for a few moments on your family. Where would you place your family on the continuums?

Family members pull together as a team.	++++|++++	Individual family members go different directions.
Family members have a strong commitment to shared values.	++++|++++	Each family member pursues own ideas.
Quality time is spent together daily.	++++|++++	Time is rarely spent together in a day.

Relationship between spouses is loving.	―++++┼++++―	Relationship between spouses is tense.
Relationship between parents and children is loving.	―++++┼++++―	Relationship between parents and children is tense.
Family has fun together regularly.	―++++┼++++―	Family rarely enjoys fun moments together.
Family atmosphere is warm, with lots of touching.	―++++┼++++―	Family atmosphere is cool, with little touching.
Family members are cooperative.	―++++┼++++―	Family members are competitive.
Family members tend to share possessions.	―++++┼++++―	Family members are highly territorial about space and possessions.
Family members regularly applaud the successes of other family members.	―++++┼++++―	Family members begrudge success of other family members.
Family communication is spontaneous, frequent, and free-flowing.	―++++┼++++―	Family communication is purely functional, sporadic, and strained.
Laughter abounds.	―++++┼++++―	Laughter is rare.
The family prays together or talks about spiritual things.	―++++┼++++―	The family rarely discusses or engages in spiritual activities.

| Problems tend to bind members together as a family. | ┼┼┼┼┼┼┼┼┼┼ | Problems tend to alienate members from one another. |

| Decisions are usually reached by consensus. | ┼┼┼┼┼┼┼┼┼┼ | Decisions are usually made by one person. |

Connect the dots with a line. Toward which edge of the continuum does your family life presently fall? Is this satisfactory to you? You may want to go back through this exercise and, with a different color pen, mark where you would consider your "ideal" family to fall on the continuums.

Check the areas you feel you need to work on to have the family life you desire:

□ Shared goals
□ Shared values
□ More time together
□ Better relationship with spouse
□ Better relationship with children
□ More fun times together
□ More hugs and touching
□ Greater affirmation, mutual support

□ Increased willingness to share space and possessions
□ Improved communication
□ Enhanced cooperation
□ More laughter
□ Deeper spiritual life as a family
□ Improved problem solving
□ Other: _____
_____

> Let us not grow weary while doing good, for in due season we shall reap if we do not lose heart. Therefore, as we have opportunity, let us do good to all, especially to those who are of the household of faith.
> —Galatians 6:9–10

Your Personal Commitment to a Stronger Family

Give serious thought to each item, and then write a response to it. Be honest with yourself, and be as objective as possible about your family.

Parents should be respected.

_____
_____

Children should be seen and not heard most of the time.

_____
_____

After vacation, I usually need a vacation from my family. Why do I feel this way?

_____

_____

I have to go outside my family to get most of my personal needs met (for feelings of fulfillment and self-worth).

_____

_____

I feel guilty because I don't spend as much time with my family as I'd like.

_____

_____

I can hardly wait until my children are grown so I can have more time to myself.

_____

_____

My children seem to be growing up so fast!

_____

_____

I'm most content in my family when

_____

_____

If I could change just one thing about my family life, it would be

_____

_____

To respond to this item, check all of the factors below that apply, but don't limit yourself to this list. The foremost obstacles to my spending more time with my family are

☐ Work demands   ☐ Different values
☐ Strained relationships   ☐ Conflicting schedules
☐ Difficult circumstances   ☐ Lack of common interests

☐ Too many other obligations

☐ Don't like some members

☐ Distance (don't live with family)

☐ Unforgiven hurts, unhealed wounds

☐ Other: _____

_____

Reflecting on Your Childhood

Pause to recall your childhood.

What did you enjoy most?

_____

_____

What were the most meaningful events in your childhood? (As an adult, you should be enjoying and succeeding at these activities, also!)

_____

_____

List the ten foremost characteristics that you would like for your children to remember as descriptive of your family life:

1. _____   6. _____
2. _____   7. _____
3. _____   8. _____
4. _____   9. _____
5. _____   10. _____

Reviewing Your Reflections

What are the five foremost things that you believe you need to do—and that you can begin to do immediately—to develop the kind of family relationships you seek to have?

1. _____
2. _____
3. _____
4. _____
5. _____

Mapping Out a Strategy

Give some thought to the specific strategies you may need to employ to reach the goals you've listed. "Spend more time together" is a possible goal. You could set aside one night a week as "Family Night." Or you could plan to have breakfast together every morning as a family. In identifying strategies, I find that it helps first to list *all* possible strategies that come to mind. Then go back over your list and highlight the strategies that will work for your family.

Goal #1
Possible strategies:

_____

_____

_____

Goal #2
Possible strategies:

_____

_____

_____

Goal #3
Possible strategies:

_____

_____

_____

Goal #4
Possible strategies:

_____

_____

_____

Goal #5
Possible strategies:

_____

_____

_____

Family Future

Families change and grow. Five years from now, your family is likely to be quite different from what it's like today. Give some thought to what your family future is likely to be.

Within Five Years

Complete each of the sentences to reflect changes you expect within the next five years.

My spouse is likely to _____ .

My child, _____ *(name)*, is likely to _____ .

My child, _____ *(name)*, is likely to _____ .

My mother *(if alive)* is likely to _____ .

My father *(if alive)* is likely to _____ .

My mother-in-law *(if alive)* is likely to _____ .

My father-in-law *(if alive)* is likely to _____ .

Overall, it is likely that our family _____
_____ .

My role in the family is likely to be that of _____ .

My Dreams and Hopes for My Family

In addition to what you can expect in real terms of added years and normal growth patterns, you undoubtedly have hopes and dreams for yourself, your spouse, and your children. Identify some here.

My dreams for my spouse include _____ .

My dreams for my child, _____ *(name)*, include _____ .

My dreams for my child, _____ (name), include _____.

My dreams for myself include _____.

My dreams for my parents include _____.

My dreams for my parents-in-law include _____.

My overall dreams and hopes for my family are _____.

Meeting Needs

Every family has needs and problems. Some of them are collective; some are related to individual family members. Identify the foremost needs facing your family in the coming twelve months.

Needs my spouse is likely to face: _____

Needs my child, _____ (name), is likely to face: _____

Needs my child, _____ (name), is likely to face: _____

Needs I am likely to face: _____

Needs my parents are likely to face: _____

Needs my parents-in-law are likely to face: _____

Overall needs our family is likely to face: _____

Reflecting on Your Family's Future

Look back over the pages related to your family's future, dreams and hopes, and needs, and ask yourself, What role can, should, or will I play in this family member's future?

In some cases, your answer will be based on what you are *expected* to do for each family member. In other cases, your answer will be drawn from what you personally *hope* to do for loved ones. In nearly all cases, however, your answer will reflect what you honestly believe you can do to help loved ones live more fulfilling lives.

■ Family Activities

You now turn your attention to the activities that bind a family together. In many cases, family activities tend to define relationships or provide opportunities for building relationships. What a family "does" is vitally linked to what a family "is."

Mutual Activities

In the box next to each item, put one check mark in box 1 if you have ever done this activity together as a family, put a second check mark in box 2 if you have done this activity during the last year, and put a third check mark in box 3 if you enjoyed the activity and would like to do it again in the future. If you have not engaged in a particular activity but think you might like to at some point in the future, put an X.

1 2 3

☐ ☐ ☐ Went to church
☐ ☐ ☐ Played a family softball, tag football, basketball, or similar outdoor game
☐ ☐ ☐ Attended a concert
☐ ☐ ☐ Prayed as a family
☐ ☐ ☐ Attended a theatrical production (play, musical, pageant)
☐ ☐ ☐ Went to a county, state, or world's fair
☐ ☐ ☐ Took a vacation together (for longer than overnight)
☐ ☐ ☐ Went on a camping trip
☐ ☐ ☐ Played board or card games
☐ ☐ ☐ Visited a gallery or museum
☐ ☐ ☐ Went hunting or fishing (or on a camera safari or bird-watching)
☐ ☐ ☐ Played together with child's toys
☐ ☐ ☐ Went to a park
☐ ☐ ☐ Rode bicycles together
☐ ☐ ☐ Went bowling, played miniature golf, or engaged in a similar activity
☐ ☐ ☐ Went to the batting range, golfing range, or other practice range
☐ ☐ ☐ Took a train trip
☐ ☐ ☐ Went to the beach
☐ ☐ ☐ Took a hike or walk in the woods
☐ ☐ ☐ Went skiing or snowmobile riding
☐ ☐ ☐ Gardened

1 2 3

☐ ☐ ☐ Built something together

☐ ☐ ☐ Attended a professional sporting event (such as baseball game, hockey game, football game)

☐ ☐ ☐ Repaired something together

☐ ☐ ☐ Went to an amusement park or theme park

☐ ☐ ☐ Attended a class together

☐ ☐ ☐ Watched movies or videos

☐ ☐ ☐ Attended a competitive exhibit (such as car show, flower show, dog show) or race (such as a marathon, car race)

☐ ☐ ☐ Went rafting or boating together

☐ ☐ ☐ Went waterskiing together

List other activities that you have enjoyed together or that you think you might enjoy doing together as a family:

_____

_____

_____

_____

_____

_____

Your Daily Routine

Coordinating a family's daily routine is no simple task. Gather your family together and pick a day and a time as your family time.

Identify that time here: _____.

Take a few minutes to evaluate your various obligations, noting which activities or commitments involve more than one member of the family.

Ask yourself these questions about your family's activities:

Are there any activities that could be dropped easily so that the family can spend more time together?

_____

Are there activities that involve one person that might also involve other members of the family?

_____

Are there any obligations that should come to an end?

_____

Are there new commitments that should be made?

_____

Make a special note of any activities that require out-of-town travel or long commutes. Do all family members make these treks? Can they? Should they? Is the commuting time necessary? What might you do to enhance family communication during travel time?

_____

_____

■ Summing Up and Setting Goals

The family was God's idea. He set up the plan. He expects us to follow it. Throughout the history of God's people, the greatest lessons to be learned are in a family context. That's also the place where we find the greatest opportunities for growth, the greatest struggles, the most intense emotions, and the deepest desires.

Your responsibility to your family is at least twofold:

1. To be the best person you can be. Who you are becomes part of the whole nature of your family. You can rise above your family background. But your present family can never rise above the moral level at which you live.
2. To relate to persons in your family with love. This love is generally expressed in terms of encouragement, presence, help in times of need, and acts of service.

When you envision standing before the Lord someday, do you envision your family by your side? Is your number one concern for the spiritual future and well-being of each of your family members? Are you willing to sacrifice some of your personal goals to see this happen?

As you reflect on your responses in this chapter, note the trends and statements that seem to be repeated. Note particularly

- areas in which you long for greater family closeness.
- your concerns for other family members.
- problems that you'd like to see resolved in your family.

Summary Statements

Write in one paragraph or less the way you feel about your family.

_____

_____

_____

_____

Write in one paragraph or less your hopes for your family.

_____

_____

_____

_____

Write in one paragraph or less the general changes you'd like to see in your family as a whole. Cite why.

_____

_____

_____

_____

How do you think your family would describe you?

_____

_____

_____

_____

Note any major recurring theme or idea that has come to you as you have worked on this chapter. Does your family have an overriding need? Does your family have a compelling drive toward a goal? Does your family have a strong identity? A sense of purpose?

_____

_____

_____

_____

If you had to write just one word or phrase to motivate yourself to more loving relationships within your family, what might that word or phrase be?

_____

Goal Statements

As you reflect on this chapter and the summary statements you have written, begin to write goals related to your family. Examples of vague and specific family goal statements are given below:

Ineffective:
Love my children more.
Spend more quality time with my spouse.

Effective:
I will spend at least a half hour a week alone with each child.
I will have a date with my spouse every Saturday night.

Your goals related to your family may be short-range, mid-range, or long-range. Note goals that you may not be able to accomplish by yourself. What might you need to do to persuade others to follow your lead in developing closer family ties?

My Family-Related Goals

Write your goals for improving your family life.

_____

_____

_____

_____

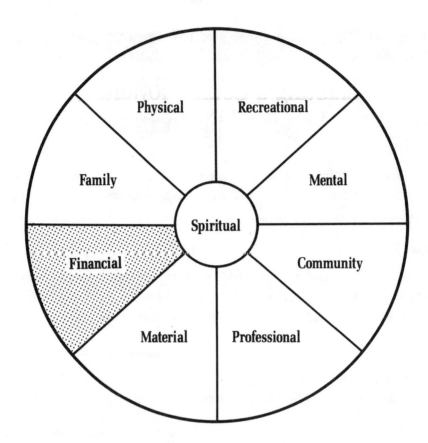

SECRET: The secret to financial success is a paradox—money is valuable only when it is saved or shared.

SCRIPTURE: "Give, and it will be given to you: good measure, pressed down, shaken together, and running over will be put into your bosom. For with the same measure that you use, it will be measured back to you" (Luke 6:38).

4

Charting a Course Toward Improved Finances

THE SCRIPTURES teach us that a *love* of money is at the root of all evil. We need to note that the emphasis here is on the *love* of money and not on money itself. We are to have a right perspective about money and recognize that it is not our source of supply but only a means to an end.

The Scriptures teach us that we are to handle money wisely. We are to use it for good, not evil.

The Scriptures teach us that we are to trust God to supply us with what we need. He bestows all wealth.

Finally, the Scriptures teach us that we are to be generous in giving away our money to persons in need. We are not to hoard our resources; we are to invest them in others for an eternal benefit to them and to us.

In this chapter, you will have an opportunity to appraise some of your ideas about money and give some thought to the ways you handle money and what you desire as a financial future. Concentrate on developing financial strategies that will allow you to do what the Lord is calling you to do and to live the way He is leading you to live.

■ Your Current Financial State

In this section you'll be thinking about various factors related to your finances—both now and in the future. You'll be dealing with perceptions about money and actual facts related to your financial condition. Be sure to keep these two approaches separate.

Deal in reality. Don't express what you hope will be your financial state or financial worth if the segment asks you to be realistic about what presently is.

Perceptions About My Financial Future

When you think about your future financial situation in comparison to your present reality, you no doubt have hopes for more. More may be in terms of quantity, quality, stability, or liquidity. At the same time, you probably have reservations about your ability to have more. As you confront your apprehensions, think about ways in which more might become a reality for you.

Obstacles to My Financial Future

What do you perceive is keeping you from a brighter financial future? Check all of the items that you believe are related to your life, and then check related items in each category or answer the related questions:

☐ **Insufficient understanding about finances, markets, and money management**

What might you do to become better informed?

☐ Read money-related magazines.   ☐ Take a course.

☐ Subscribe to an investment newsletter.   ☐ Regularly read the financial section of the newspaper.

☐ Join an investors group.   ☐ Hire a money manager.

☐ Order a course on cassette tape related to a particular area of investment.   ☐ Work with a broker.

☐ Ask friends or relatives for advice.

☐ Watch money-related TV shows.   ☐ Other: _____

☐ Consult an expert.   _____

☐ **Insufficient capital**

How much do you believe you need? _____

Where can you get the capital you desire?

☐ Borrow it.
From whom? _____   ☐ Seek additional investors.
Who? _____

_____   _____

DREAM A LITTLE DREAM:
Holding the Keys to God's Storehouse of Supply

Take a few minutes to imagine that you have been given the keys to God's store-house. In it is all the wealth of the universe. Your eyes are dazzled by the glint of jewels and precious metals. They make the sound of wind chimes as they spill out of vats from which they continually seem to be created. You have been given permission to take whatever you want, as much as you want, and to use it in any way that you want.

   Put yourself in the scene. What feelings do you have? What do you say? What do you decide to take? How much do you take? What do you do with it?

   Write freely as thoughts and images come to your mind:

_____
_____
_____
_____
_____
_____
_____
_____
_____
_____
_____
_____
_____
_____
_____
_____
_____
_____
_____
_____
_____
_____
_____
_____
_____
_____
_____

What is the possibility of your seeing a positive rate of return on this additional money? _____

How much additional capital might you be able to earn (being very conservative and taking into consideration the possibility of unforeseen events or circumstances)? _____

How much capital might you lose if this venture fails? _____

How much additional capital might you be able to set aside from present earnings (through readjustment of your budget)? _____

☐ **Bad economic times**

Why is this a bad economic time for your particular service or the product you produce? _____
_____
_____

Is the problem primarily related to one of these factors?

☐ Your family or personal situation

☐ Your perception of the national economy

☐ Your city's or community's current economic situation

☐ Your company's current financial situation

☐ Your industry's current financial situation

☐ Other: _____
_____

Circle the problem areas in which you have some degree of control or influence. What might you be able to do in each of these areas to improve economic conditions? _____
_____
_____

Do you anticipate a time when the current economic downturn will be resolved? _____ If so, when? _____

What is your strategy for enduring this current economic downturn? _____
_____
_____

☐ **Poor credit rating**

What can you do to improve your credit rating? _____

_____

Have you taken a long, hard look as to how you earned a poor credit rating? ____
Have you taken steps to turn around this situation or habit? _____

If so, what are they?

_____

_____

(See the questions related to debt later in this section.)

If your poor credit rating is related to bankruptcy, how many years remain before you are able to reestablish a good credit rating? _____

> What is your strategy for sound financial management during this interim period? _____
>
> _____
>
> What changes are you making in your finances so that you will have sound financial management practices in place when you emerge from bankruptcy?
>
> _____
>
> _____

☐ **Inflation rate**

What is the present inflation rate? _____
What inflation rate do you believe is necessary to your financial growth? _____
When do you anticipate that such an inflation rate may be in place? _____
Based on what information?_____

Is there anything you can do to prepare for that change, effect that change, or better anticipate when that change might occur? _____

_____

Investors in overseas currencies are frequently concerned about policies related to inflation rates in the countries for which they are holding funds. If this is your situation, what sources of information are you relying on as indicators of change in inflation rates? _____

_____

☐ Taxes

What might you do to decrease your level of taxation?

- ☐ Consult a tax attorney.
- ☐ Read more about tax-deferred investments.
- ☐ Complete tax estimates in sufficient time to make beneficial adjustments.
- ☐ Have taxes prepared by a professional.
- ☐ Work closely with a tax accountant.
- ☐ Research ways in which to lower taxes.
- ☐ Other: _____
  _____
  _____
  _____

How much time (and money) are you willing to devote to means of lowering your taxes? _____

What do you believe the benefits of this expenditure of time and money might be? _____

☐ In wrong job

A job may be wrong for a number of reasons. Perhaps it doesn't have enough rewards attached to it or enough room for growth and advancement. Perhaps it is ill-suited to your talents, skills, experience, or desires. Perhaps it is problematic—owing to personnel, equipment, or scheduling difficulties. Before moving to a new job, you may want to evaluate what you *don't* like about your present one.

Why do you believe you are presently in the wrong job?

- ☐ No possibility of advancement
- ☐ No possibility for increase in remuneration
- ☐ Insufficient training for job
- ☐ Overskilled for job
- ☐ Sales down
- ☐ Excessive expectations for performance
- ☐ Inequities
- ☐ Too long a commute
- ☐ Strong family disapproval
- ☐ Work not fulfilling or not motivating
- ☐ Work unsuited to talents, skills, or abilities
- ☐ Cutbacks or layoffs planned
- ☐ Scheduling difficulties
- ☐ Personality conflicts
- ☐ Discrimination
- ☐ Too much stress
- ☐ Other: _____
  _____

What can you do to find a better job?

□ Check ads.
□ Network with friends.
□ Get additional training.
□ Ask for transfer within current company.
□ Get part-time job in other area.
□ Talk to job-finding agency.
□ Send out resumes.

□ Make calls to businesses for which you think you'd like to work.
□ Discuss situation with boss.
□ Take lessons (or enter an apprenticeship).
□ Other: _____

How soon can you start taking action to get a better job? _____
By what date would you like to move into a better job? _____

What might you do to ensure that you leave your present job with the best reputation possible? _____
_____
_____

□ In wrong profession

Why do you believe you are in the wrong profession?

□ Profession is becoming obsolete.
□ Work is not fulfilling.
□ Market is saturated.
□ Profession is not truly suited to personal aptitudes.
□ Expectations for performance can't be met.
□ Rewards are inadequate.
□ Respected persons offered that advice.

□ Too many people are presently in this profession.
□ Anticipated expenses are rising faster than anticipated income.
□ Interests have changed.
□ Stress is excessive.
□ Opportunity for personal growth is lacking.
□ Aptitude testing indicated it.
□ Other: _____

What might you do to change professions?

□ Seek specialized training.
□ Take aptitude test to discover true talents.

□ Talk to experts or workers in other fields.
□ Get additional schooling.

☐ Read about work in other professions.

☐ Take on part-time job or enter an apprenticeship to try a new field.

☐ Other: _____

_____

_____

How soon can you begin to pursue a new profession? _____

What time frame are you considering for making a change in your profession?

_____

☐ Restrictive company policies

What policies do you believe are holding you back professionally or financially?

_____

_____

What might you do to bring about a positive, constructive change in these policies?

_____

_____

☐ Uncooperative boss

In what ways do you believe your current boss is uncooperative?

☐ Inflexible   ☐ Uncommunicative

☐ Intolerant   ☐ Power hungry

☐ Indecisive   ☐ Harasses

☐ Abusive   ☐ Not open to ideas

☐ Requires perfection   ☐ Other: _____

☐ Discriminates   _____

What might you do to help your boss overcome these relational obstacles? Are there ways in which you might be a better communicator or improve your performance level? _____

_____

Is there a possibility of transferring to an area in which you believe you might work for someone who is a better boss? _____

What makes you think this boss will be better? _____

_____

☐ Uncooperative spouse

In what specific ways do you believe your spouse is an obstacle to a brighter financial future?

☐ Spends too much money.
☐ Gives away too much money.
☐ Has limited money management skills (such as budget making, checkbook balancing).
☐ Refuses to relocate.
☐ Won't participate in company events or travel.
☐ Won't consolidate finances.
☐ Spends money unwisely.

☐ Refuses to talk about money.
☐ Has different financial goals.
☐ Has never earned own money.
☐ Is dishonest about money.
☐ Resents job demands.
☐ Refuses to participate in financial planning.
☐ Discourages working.
☐ Other: _____

_____

What might you do to bypass or bring about a change in any of these areas you have identified as an obstacle? _____

_____

_____

_____

☐ Personal debt

You may very well feel that debt is your number one obstacle to a brighter financial future. Remember these seven keys as you begin to tackle debt:

1. Devise a realistic debt-reduction plan.
2. Pay cash.
3. Resolve to stick with your plan.
4. Curtail current spending levels in order to have more to pay against your debt.
5. Identify any areas in which you can give yourself a jump start in reducing your indebtedness.
6. Resist the urge to spend in an area that you've freed of debt.
7. Don't take on debt assuming that things will get better in your life (or that you will get a raise, earn more money, come into a windfall of some type, and so forth).

Current Debt Load

What is your current debt load? List all items that require regular payment. If you have a quarterly or annual payment, divide that amount into monthly payments here.

	Total	Monthly Payment
Home mortgage:		
Amount remaining on vehicle purchase (list all vehicles):		
Land or property purchase:		
School loans:		
Personal or consolidation loans (list all):		
Credit card debt (list all):		
Other payments (such as back taxes):		
Total:		

Current Periodic Financial Obligations

In addition to payments against indebtedness (at the conclusion of which you will have enacted full payment for an item), you probably have periodic financial obligations: leases, insurance premium payments, rental fees, maintenance fees, base prices for utilities and telephone service, and so forth. Taxes and social security payments should be considered periodic financial obligations, even if they are routinely deducted from a paycheck.

List all of your periodic financial obligations. (If you have annual periodic payments, break them down into monthly amounts.)

Item	Monthly Amount
Taxes:	
Federal	_____
State	_____
Other	_____
Social security payments:	_____
Health insurance:	_____
Life insurance:	_____
Leases, rental fees, base payments, maintenance fees, and so forth (list all):	
_____	_____
_____	_____
_____	_____
_____	_____
_____	_____
_____	_____
Total:	_____

Now add the total monthly amount you are paying against indebtedness and the total monthly amount you are paying for periodic financial obligations.

Grand Total: _____

What percentage of your total income is this amount? _____
Are you surprised at the amount or the percentage? _____

What steps can you take to reduce your indebtedness?

_____

_____

_____

Which periodic financial obligations might you work to lower or eliminate (perhaps until your indebtedness is decreased or eliminated)? List them, with the amount you believe you can save to apply against indebtedness:

_____

_____

_____

_____

The Stress of Debt

You may assume from the previous pages that I'm advocating a no-debt lifestyle. You're right. The freest, most enjoyable way to live is to live without indebtedness.

I'm also realistic enough to know that very few people live a no-debt lifestyle or will be able to achieve that lifestyle in a short period of time.

I do make these assumptions:

- You *can* achieve a no-debt lifestyle.
- You *can* live with minimal debt until you achieve a no-debt lifestyle.
- From time to time, a person may find it advantageous to enter into debt (for example, to start a business or purchase a home). The goal of entering into any form of debt, however, should be coupled with a goal of getting out of debt with real property marked "paid in full."

Anytime you make a decision to enter into debt, ask yourself,

- How many years will it take me to pay off this amount?
- Can I reduce the number of years it will take to pay off the amount? (You may be able to switch from a thirty-year mortgage, for example, to a fifteen-year mortgage.) If so, what will be the added monthly payment?
- Will I own something that has increased in value (or has the potential to increase in value) when I have completed this purchase?

Also take a look at the potential toll that debt is placing on your life and on loved ones.

	Low Impact	*High Impact*
Does your indebtedness influence the amount of stress you feel?		
Has your indebtedness affected your overall health and sense of well-being?		
Has your indebtedness affected your relationships (family, friends)?		
Does your indebtedness have an impact on your spiritual life?		
Has your indebtedness affected the amount of time you spend on recreation and antistress activities (negatively or positively)?		

Finally, ask yourself this question about debt and the stress it can cause: Is it possible that I have fallen into a pattern of spending more money on things to help me reduce the stress I feel that is related to indebtedness? (Some people go on buying sprees after confronting their debt load; others join expensive health clubs to counteract stress directly related to their overspending; still others opt for consolidation loans that can increase their debt burden over time with high interest rates.)

_____

_____

_____

_____

■ Your Attitudes About Money

To have a good baseline profile as you begin your life planning process, you need to have a clear understanding of your habits and views regarding money and financial security.

General Financial Values

Respond to each of the value statements below with a "yes" or "no" answer.

	Yes	No
I believe it's important to live within my means.	☐	☐
I believe it's a good idea to live debt-free.	☐	☐
I believe an individual should be fully responsible for personal debts.	☐	☐
I believe it's a good idea to save money on a regular basis.	☐	☐
I believe every person should have a retirement fund to which regular payments are made.	☐	☐
I believe it's important to make regular charitable contributions to worthwhile organizations and projects.	☐	☐
I believe credit cards should be used only in an emergency.	☐	☐
I pay off the full amount of all my charge accounts each month.	☐	☐
I believe a person should invest money (in real property for long-term growth) on a regular basis.	☐	☐

Take a long look at any "no" answers. Why do you hold those opinions?

_____

_____

_____

_____

Spending Values

	Yes	No
I routinely overspend.	☐	☐
I have greater debt today than I had this time last year.	☐	☐
I need help from someone else to meet my monthly financial obligations.	☐	☐
I routinely save money.	☐	☐
I have a retirement account.	☐	☐
I routinely contribute money to worthy causes and organizations.	☐	☐
I routinely use credit cards in paying for items.	☐	☐
I rarely pay off the full amount I charge in any given month.	☐	☐
I routinely invest money.	☐	☐

Take a long look at any "yes" answers. Now compare your financial values and your spending values. Do you believe one thing and do another? What might you do to adjust your habits?

_____

_____

_____

_____

■ Taking a Risk

How willing are you to take a risk when it comes to money or investments?

How much of a risk taker are you willing to be in pursuing your career or in starting your own business?

In evaluating risk, take a look at how much risk you presently face and then how much you are willing to put at risk.

Anticipating the Probability of Change

How do you answer the following questions on a risk scale? Indicate your responses with check marks.

	Degree of Probability		
	Low	Medium	High
What is the likelihood that I will be in the same position I hold today this time next year?			
What is the likelihood of my job being eliminated during the coming year?			
What is the likelihood of my being fired or released for lack of performance during the coming year?			
What is the likelihood that my company will merge with another company during the coming year?			

	Degree of Probability		
	Low	Medium	High
What is the likelihood that my current office or department will be consolidated with another office or department during the coming year?			
What is the likelihood that I might be sued during the coming year for failure to perform or for failure of the performance of a product I produce?			
What is the likelihood that I will have a lower income this time next year?			

Look at the various marks. Ask yourself,

What is the overall trend? _____

As a whole, am I facing a high-risk year ahead? _____

Is this level of risk stressful or something to worry about? _____

Now answer the questions related to a longer time period.

	Degree of Probability		
	Low	Medium	High
What is the likelihood that I will be in the same position I hold today for the rest of my career?			
What is the likelihood of my job being eliminated at some point in my life?			
What is the likelihood of my being fired or released for lack of performance at some point in my career?			

	Degree of Probability		
	Low	Medium	High
What is the likelihood that my company will merge with another company at some point in the future?			
What is the likelihood that my current office or department will be consolidated with another office or department at some time in the future?			
What is the likelihood that I might be sued at some point in the future for failure to perform or for failure of the performance of a product I produce?			
What is the likelihood that I will have a lower income at some point in the future?			

Again, look at the marks. Then respond to these questions:

What is the overall risk level I am facing in the indefinite future? _____
Do I find this troublesome? _____

How do my responses to the near-future risk levels and the long-term risk levels compare? _____
_____
_____
_____
_____
_____

In facing the near future, what have I done to minimize the trauma that change may bring to my life? _____
_____
_____
_____

What more might I do? _____

_____

_____

_____

In facing the long term, what have I done to minimize the trauma of change?

_____

_____

_____

What more might I do? _____

_____

_____

_____

_____

Areas of Risk Taking

In addition to evaluating risk in short-term and long-term time frames, take a look at the areas of your life you are willing to put at risk.

	Willingness to Change	
	Yes	No
Are you willing to risk losing your job in asking for a new assignment or an increase in compensation?	☐	☐
Are you willing to resign from your job in pursuit of a new job or career?	☐	☐
Do you require a bird in the hand before making a move?	☐	☐
Are you willing to change your profession to pursue a career you think will be more fulfilling, productive, or stable in the future?	☐	☐

Who Is Taking the Risk?

In evaluating risk, identify who, other than you, may be asked to participate in the risk. Ask,

Does the risk related to an investment or a job move affect any other person? ____
If so, who? In what ways? _____

_____

How is that person (or people) likely to respond to change or increased risk?

_____

_____

Am I willing to risk destroying or damaging my relationship with this person (or
these people) in pursuing a change that brings unwanted tension and increased
risk? _____

■ Your Own Business

Not only do you need to find the right niche for your talents, skills, experience,
and education, but you need to find the right niche in which you can be best
rewarded.

Many people limit their financial future by *not* considering the possibility of
going into business for themselves. Others fail to consider all of the options that
might be negotiated in their work for others. Still others may find that their greatest
financial rewards lie within the framework of a large or small company.

Take stock of your desire and ability to be an entrepreneur. Check each trait
under the column that best reflects your response.

	Poor	Good	Outstanding
Ability to make decisions			
Take responsibility for the decisions I make			
Ability to follow through on plans			
Flexibility in hours			
Expectation of immediate success			

	Poor	Good	Outstanding
Sufficient time to devote to start-up of business			
Family support			
Ability to live with irregular cash flow			
Willing to do wide variety of tasks related to business			
Desire for quick cash return			
Capable of doing diverse tasks related to business			
Capable of managing money			
Like working with people			
Expectation of financial success in near future			
Have unique product or service to fit unique market niche			
Good communication skills (both listening and talking)			
A desire to meet needs or to help others			
Ability to meet deadlines			
Place value on quality over quantity			
Good knowledge of profession			
Solid ability in profession			
Experience in profession			
Good time-management skills			

	Poor	Good	Outstanding
Have good network of associates and advisors			
Understanding of customer needs			
Desire to work hard			
Have start-up capital in hand (or can acquire it)			
Flexibility in making midcourse corrections			
Willingness to ask for help			
Able to identify areas of weakness			
Quality control mechanisms			

State in fifty words or less what service or product you would like to offer the public (which is not currently being offered or which you believe you could offer with better quality or price).

_____

_____

_____

_____

_____

Reflect on the statement you have written and your answers to the self-evaluation above. Look for these essentials:

- Quality of service or product you intend to render
- Pricing (of your service or product to be competitive)
- A unique approach to providing your service, or unique aspects of your product
- A unique need in the marketplace for your service or product
- A willingness to work long, hard hours with very few initial rewards

Be wary of a desire to get rich quick or to think that a business of your own is a way to have more leisure time with fewer responsibilities. A business of your own is likely to be highly time consuming and demanding of all your resources (intellectual, emotional, financial, and physical).

Before pursuing a business of your own, consider these issues:

Who will buy your product or service? (Be able to state in twenty-five to fifty words the profile of the customer you intend to serve.)

_____

_____

_____

_____

What will customers like most about your product or service?

_____

_____

_____

_____

Why will they want to continue doing business with you (after an initial contact)?

_____

_____

_____

_____

Who can help you in your business and in what ways? (List as many resources as you can. Highlight in some way persons from whom you can count on major help or support.)

_____

_____

_____

_____

Finally, ask yourself these key questions related to starting your own business:

When is the best time to launch this business?

_____

_____

_____

_____

Should I start the business on a full-time or part-time basis? (Identify the advantages and disadvantages of both approaches.)

_____

_____

_____

_____

Where is the ideal place to set up my business? (Consider region of the country, city, neighborhood, building, home.)

_____

_____

_____

_____

■ Your Foremost Asset: YOU

YOU are your foremost asset. Take stock of what you bring to any work environment—your own business or your employment by others. The service you are able to provide, or the work you are capable of doing, is the base on which your ability to earn money rests.

Identify your money-earning talents, skills, education, experience, and motivational traits. Be generous, but be honest, in appraising yourself.

This section is closely related to forms and exercises you will find in chapter 6. These items are placed here as a means of directing your attention to your traits and interests as they relate to your ability to earn, spend, or talk about money. Keep finances at the forefront of your thinking as you respond.

Talents (those things that you are capable of doing or seem naturally to be good at doing—include aptitudes such as "able to understand what people mean even if they don't communicate well," "ability to calculate and do math problems easily," "ability to restore things to working order," "ability to ask the right questions," and so forth):

_____

_____

_____

_____

_____

_____

Skills (those things that you can do because you have been trained to do them or have trained yourself to do them):

_____

_____

_____

_____

_____

_____

Education (those things that you have learned or degrees you have earned—include formal schooling, training courses, specialized seminars, and self-constructed courses):

_____

_____

_____

_____

_____

_____

Experience (those things that you have done—include volunteer and work-related positions):

_____

_____

_____

_____

_____

_____

_____

_____

Motivational traits (your desire to do, experience, accomplish, and be more in the future than you are today).

Ask yourself such questions as these:

- How hard do I really want to work to make more money?
- How willing am I to make changes in my earning and spending habits?
- Do I have a strong definition of financial success?
- Am I willing to go an extra mile for another person or to give extra effort to a project whether there's financial reward or not? Am I more motivated to give more time and energy if there's potential for a bonus or raise?
- Am I willing to sacrifice some things to achieve my financial goals? And what am I willing to sacrifice?
- What really motivates me to earn money?
- What captivates my interest the most when it comes to money?
- Do I need continual prodding, or am I self-motivated to do a job that I see needs doing?
- How dependent am I on the praise and tangible rewards given by others?
- Do I learn from my financial failures and mistakes?
- Do I make midcourse corrections quickly and wisely when I see that I'm heading for a financial disaster?
- Am I willing to learn something new, including something new about money, investing, and financial management?
- Do I have a strong value system that I refuse to compromise, no matter how much money may be involved?
- Am I quick to see new financial opportunities?
- Do I see things as financial challenges or problems?
- What disappoints me the most about my finances?

This list is by no means comprehensive. You'll think of others as you reflect on what motivates you. List your positive motivational traits:

_____
_____
_____
_____
_____
_____

Specific Capabilities

Although you may have listed some of these skills on the previous pages, make sure that you have identified as many *specific* capabilities as possible. Include items that may seem more related to your hobbies or to life's routines than to your work. Capabilities tend to overlap, even if you aren't aware of them. (Remember that you are focusing on capabilities that may have financial ramifications.)

What languages do you speak, including computer languages? (Include any specialized dialects.) Indicate next to each language your level of proficiency.

_____
_____
_____

Are you adept at using the specialized vocabulary of a particular field? If so, which field(s)?

_____
_____
_____

What machines are you adept at using?

_____
_____
_____

What hand tools are you skilled at using?

_____
_____
_____

Specific Interests

You may have identified some of these things under education or talents, but if not, note them here. (Again, these are interests that may have financial implications.)

Reading interests (types of books you've read the most in recent years):

_____

_____

_____

Listening interests (types of tapes, records, compact discs, or performances you've heard the most in recent years):

_____

_____

_____

Performance interests (types of events you've attended the most in recent years—including lectures, plays, movies, concerts, sporting events):

_____

_____

_____

Activity interests (types of things you've enjoyed doing most in your leisure time—including jogging, doing needlepoint, giving dinner parties):

_____

_____

_____

You may be asking, "What does this have to do with work?" Take a look at what you have jotted down. Have you listed "work" as one of your activity interests? Did you list work-related books or tapes among your reading or listening interests?

_____

_____

_____

_____

If not, why not? Is it possible that you are more interested in nonwork topics and activities than you are in your work? Should you consider a career change so that you are operating more in your area of interest or ability?

_____

_____

_____

Communication Skills on the Job and in Talking About Money

Certain communication skills are vital to your work, career, and financial success. Begin to evaluate your ability by responding to each question below.

	Never	Sometimes	Always
Are you able to talk freely to your supervisor (for example, about a new idea, a need in your area, a personal request)?			
Are you able to talk freely with your colleagues?			
Are you able to talk freely with people you supervise?			
Are you able to talk freely with your customers, vendors, or people not in your immediate work area?			
Are you able to communicate well over the telephone?			
Are you able to express your ideas in written form?			
Are you able to talk freely in front of small groups?			
Are you able to talk freely in front of large groups?			
Can you think on your feet?			

	Never	Sometimes	Always
Are you good at brainstorming new ideas?			
Are you able to talk freely about work-related ideas?			
Are you able to talk freely about non-work-related ideas?			
Are you learning new vocabulary words?			
Are you learning a new language (including computer language)?			
Are you adept at using the jargon associated with your work?			
Are you good at listening?			
Do you have an ability to ask astute questions?			
Do you have an ability to prioritize ideas in expressing yourself?			
Do you have an ability to get to the main point quickly in expressing yourself?			
Do you communicate well in high-pressure situations?			
Do others ask you a lot of questions?			
Can you tolerate silence?			
Are you good at reading body language?			
Do you look up information you don't know in reference books?			
Are you afraid to ask questions?			
Do you have an ability to categorize ideas and topics?			

	Never	Sometimes	Always
Does anyone ever correct your grammar?			
Are you adept at juggling visual aids as you speak?			
Are you able to identify communication errors in others?			
Are you able to identify communication errors in yourself?			
Are you good at remembering names, dates, and faces?			
Do you have difficulty talking to strangers?			
Are you uncomfortable talking about topics vital to your work success?			
Do you understand your accountant?			
Can you ask intelligent questions about money management?			
Do you understand your banker, investment broker, or real estate agent?			
Can you ask intelligent questions about financial investments?			

People who are successful in their fields tend to be good communicators. Ask yourself,

What can I do to improve my vocabulary, especially my financial vocabulary?

☐ Read more.
☐ Take a vocabulary-building course.
☐ Regularly take the *Reader's Digest* vocabulary quiz.
☐ Look up words I hear but can't define or use properly.

☐ Ask others to define words I don't know.
☐ Buy a vocabulary-building calendar.
☐ Other: _____
_____

What more can I do to improve my general communication skills?

- ☐ Tape-record my speech and analyze it.
- ☐ Take a communication class.
- ☐ Join a Toastmasters Club.
- ☐ Videotape my presentation and self-analyze it.
- ☐ Use an editor for my written work and written speeches.
- ☐ Have a professional analysis conducted of my speaking.

- ☐ Have a professional analysis conducted of my writing.
- ☐ Ask others to correct me when I make errors.
- ☐ Rehearse more for my public presentations.
- ☐ Other: _____
  _____
  _____
  _____

■ Your Present Financial Status

How much are you worth? Your worth in terms of loving relationships and human traits cannot be calculated, of course. We're speaking here strictly of your financial worth.

Even if you have just started a career, or even if you are still in school, you have a net worth. Taking stock of your current financial position is the place to start in evaluating where you stand financially, which you must know before you make plans about where you want to be!

Your Net Worth

As you list your financial assets, you may need to add categories to the work sheet. Include all of your assets at the value they presently hold (as opposed to what you paid for them).

Checking accounts(s): _____
Savings account(s): _____
Certificates of deposit: _____
Stocks and bonds (both listed and unlisted): _____
Property (real estate): _____
Currency (including metal bullion or coins): _____
Other investments (such as antiques or art, at current
    appraisal value): _____

Value of vehicles, furnishings, and personal
   possessions (if you were to sell them today):   _____
Cash value of insurance policies or tax-deferred
   retirement accounts (should you liquidate them
   today):   _____

                                            Total: _____

Refer to your debt work sheet. State the amount
   of your total indebtedness here: _____

Subtract your indebtedness from your total assets.

                                        Net Worth: _____

Your Credit Rating

A part of your financial status is your ability to borrow money or buy items on time. This directly relates to your credit rating. Do you know your current credit rating?

You have a legal right to know what creditors may have entered into your financial files.

■ Starting with a Desire to Give

I am 100 percent convinced that a desire to give lies within each person. There's nothing more satisfying than giving, especially when the gift is made with a pure heart, for right reasons, and when the gift meets a need or solves a problem.

Generous contributions are noted throughout the Scriptures. We are admonished to give with a cheerful heart, to give in a way that the left hand doesn't know what the right hand is doing, and to make our gifts as to the Lord, expecting nothing from others in return.

The Old Testament understanding of giving was the tithe, or one-tenth, which was to be given *first*. The tithe was used to meet the needs of God's house (which we would recognize today as the church) and to meet the needs of the Levites (who, in our culture today, would not only be spiritual ministers but also those who minister to the material, physical, and emotional needs of people). The entire land was blessed by the distribution of tithes and offerings. This giving included a variety of expressions, including leaving crops for poor people to glean and distributing the excess to people in need. The number *ten* has a meaning in Hebrew: "increase." The giving of the tithe was always associated with blessing and increase for God's people.

The New Testament understanding of giving seems to be that *everything* we have belongs to God. We are to give with generous measure to further the extension of His kingdom, and to meet the needs of our brothers and sisters in Christ. Our giving level is to be determined in prayer, relying on the inspiration of the Holy Spirit. We must never misrepresent our giving.

As you reflect on your finances, ask yourself,

How much am I willing to give to the work of the Lord? _____

_____

Why is it important for me to give money to the Lord? _____

_____

_____

What other means of tangible giving might I explore as I make my contribution to the church? _____

_____

_____

_____

Allow for giving in your financial planning!

■ Making a Budget that Allows You to Grow Financially

Refer back to your debt work sheets as you prepare for this budget exercise.

Current Budget

Your total monthly income:
   (If your monthly pay fluctuates, divide last year's
      income by 12.)   Line A $_____

Your monthly financial obligations:
(Refer to the total of your fixed monthly
    payments from your debt work sheet.)   Line B $_____

Estimate your monthly expenses for life's
    necessities, such as food, utilities and
    transportation.   Line C $_____

Total Monthly Expenses (B + C) $_____

The amount remaining from your income after your expenses have been paid is often referred to as disposable income, and is disposed of immediately by most people. We prefer to call it discretionary or investment income.

Your investment income:
Subtract (B + C) from Line A   Line D $_____

Designate a monthly amount for an emergency
    fund easily accessible in a savings account.   Line E $_____

Designate a monthly amount for your long-range
    financial security and retirement.   Line F $_____

Designate a monthly amount for your church and
    philanthropic contributions.   Line G $_____

Designate a monthly amount for your growth and
    development such as education, leisure, and
    physical fitness activities.   Line H $_____

Designate a monthly amount for gifts and activities
    to enhance your personal relationships.   Line I $_____

Balance the amounts in E, F, G, H, and I so that
    their sum total equals that of Line D. $_____

To increase the amount for positive investment in your future and in the lives of loved ones, you obviously need to make adjustments in either your income or your expenses.

Using the same exercise you have just completed, envision three additional ideal budgets for yourself: one that reflects where you would like to be a year from now, five years from now, and at retirement age.

Ideal Budget for Next Year

Your projected monthly income: Line A $_____

Your projected monthly obligations:
  Fixed monthly payments   Line B $_____

  Estimated expenses for life's necessities such
    as food, utilities, and transportation   Line C $_____

Total Projected Monthly Expenses (B + C) $_____

Your investment income:
  Subtract (B + C) from Line A   Line D $_____

Invest in your peace of mind:
  Emergency Fund   Line E $_____

Invest in your financial future:
  Retirement Fund   Line F $_____

Invest in your church or community:
  Philanthropic Fund   Line G $_____

Invest in your personal growth:
  Personal Fund   Line H $_____

Invest in relationships:
  Relationship Fund   Line I $_____

Balance the amounts in E, F, G, H, and I so that
  their sum equals that of Line D. $_____

Ideal Budget for Five Years from Now

Your projected monthly income: Line A $_____

Your projected monthly obligations:
  Fixed monthly payments   Line B $_____

Estimated expenses for life's necessities such
    as food, utilities, and transportation   Line C $_____

Total Projected Monthly Expenses (B + C) $_____

Your investment income:
    Subtract (B + C) from Line A   Line D $_____

Invest in your peace of mind:
    Emergency Fund   Line E $_____

Invest in your financial future:
    Retirement Fund   Line F $_____

Invest in your church or community:
    Philanthropic Fund   Line G $_____

Invest in your personal growth:
    Personal Fund   Line H $_____

Invest in your relationships:
    Relationship Fund   Line I $_____

Balance the amounts in E, F, G, H, and I so that
    their sum equals that of Line D. $_____

Ideal Budget at Retirement

Your projected monthly income: Line A $_____

Your projected monthly obligations:
    Fixed monthly payments   Line B $_____

Estimated expenses for life's necessities such
    as food, utilities, and transportation   Line C $_____

Total Projected Monthly Expenses (B + C) $_____

Your investment income:
    Subtract (B + C) from Line A   Line D $_____

Invest in your peace of mind:
    Emergency Fund   Line E $_____

Invest in your financial future:
   Retirement Fund   Line F $_____

Invest in your church or community:
   Philanthropic Fund   Line G $_____

Invest in your personal growth:
   Personal Fund   Line H $_____

Invest in your relationships:
   Relationship Fund   Line I $_____

Balance the amounts in E, F, G, H, and I so that
   their sum equals that of Line D. $_____

Reflect on the budgets you have made:

Compare your ideal budgets with your current budget. What observations stand out to you? _____

_____

_____

_____

_____

What changes are you going to need to make in your income and/or spending?

_____

_____

_____

_____

■ Summing Up and Setting Goals

People often say, "Money talks." What has this chapter said to you about your finances, your priorities regarding money, and your future desires related to debt reduction, business opportunity, and job improvement?

As you look back over this chapter, identify specifically

- areas in which you truly believe you can make a positive step forward in your finances.
- things you can do to increase your net worth.
- ways in which you need to readjust your spending habits.
- your desires related to giving.

Summary Statements

Write in one paragraph or less your feelings about money, giving, saving, investing, budgeting—in sum, financial management.

_____
_____
_____
_____

Write in one paragraph or less the degree to which you feel that you have control over your finances—including what you earn and spend.

_____
_____
_____
_____

Write in one paragraph or less your worries about money.

_____
_____
_____
_____

Write in one paragraph or less what you would do if you suddenly had a major financial windfall. Indicate the amount unexpectedly received and what you would do with it. _____
_____
_____
_____

Reflect on what you have just written. What would keep you from handling your current level of income in a proportionate way?

_____

_____

_____

_____

Note any recurring theme or thought as you worked on this chapter.

_____

_____

_____

_____

If you had just one word or phrase to motivate yourself toward wiser financial management, what would it be? _____

_____

_____

Goal Statements

Look again through this chapter, and reread your summary statements. Now is the time to make specific goals about your finances. Remember that these goal statements are to reflect what you actually desire and are willing to do.

Examples of vague/ineffective and specific/effective financial goal statements are given below:

Ineffective:
Stay out of debt.
Save more money.

Effective:
I will not spend more than I earn.
I will save 8 percent of my salary this year and put all bonus checks into an investment account.

Your goals related to your finances should include short-range, mid-range, or long-range goals. Some of your goals may relate to other people, such as a spouse. Note the goals that you may *not* be able to accomplish by yourself.

My Financial Goals

Write your goals for improving your finances.

_____

_____

_____

_____

_____

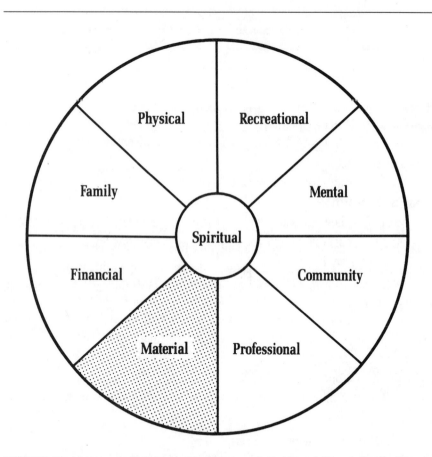

SECRET: Buy it new; wear it out. Fix it up, or do without. An uncluttered home helps you lead an uncluttered life.

SCRIPTURE: "But lay up for yourselves treasures in heaven, where neither moth nor rust destroys and where thieves do not break in and steal. For where your treasure is, there your heart will be also" (Matt. 6:20–21).

Taking Stock of
Your Stuff

IN THE STORY of Heidi, the young girl went to her grandfather's chalet in the Alps dressed in layer upon layer of clothing. She literally took everything she owned on her back.

Many of today's backpackers make a similar claim: "I'm carrying everything I need with me."

Most of us, however, carry very little of what we own with us—most of what we possess is generally around us, parked in a garage, or filed in a portfolio of papers tucked away in a vault.

Much of life—our time, our concern, our effort—is spent in the acquisition and maintenance of stuff, our material things. We shop for stuff, store stuff (usually in other stuff), clean stuff, use stuff, and discard stuff virtually every day of our lives. And yet, such a major part of life is rarely planned. Many of us are impulse buyers and sellers of goods. Many fail to use items once they are purchased or to maintain them properly.

Here is your opportunity to take stock of your stuff and to plan your future acquisitions and management of personal goods.

■ An Evaluation of Your Dwelling

It is a good idea at least once a year to give your house, or houses, a thorough assessment. My wife and I set aside one day a year for evaluating our house and yard. On that day we make a master list of everything that needs repair, replacement, or refurbishing.

As you assess the condition of your dwelling and yard, look for items such as these. Check off those that need attention:

☐ Structural problems (exterior, such as sagging porch)	☐ Structural problems (interior, such as cracks in wall)
☐ Plumbing problems	☐ Electrical problems
☐ Paint	☐ Wallpaper
☐ Dead or dying plants	☐ Swimming pool, spa, or tennis court
☐ Floor coverings	
☐ Lighting fixtures	☐ Fences and borders
☐ Lawn or ground cover	☐ Retaining walls
☐ Condition of wood	☐ Condition of plaster
☐ Roof	☐ Walkways, driveway
☐ Windows	☐ Bathroom fixtures
☐ Cabinets and built-ins	☐ Stairs
☐ Fireplace	☐ Water heater(s)
☐ Heating units	☐ Air-conditioning units
☐ Ductwork	☐ Tile

Don't forget the attic, basement, garage, and storage sheds. In addition to your primary dwelling, you'll want to conduct the same inventory for your vacation home(s) and any rented storage spaces.

Using a small notebook or separate sheets of paper, write the room or area of your house that you are evaluating and then next to it the items that need repair or replacement, your time frame for doing the repair or replacement, and the estimated cost.

■ Capital Improvements

Are you planning to remodel your kitchen or enclose your porch to create a garden room? Are you hoping to install ceiling fans or add solar panels? Use this list for any major capital improvements you hope to make to your dwelling(s). Consider these items as you make your list:

☐ Additions	☐ Deck or terrace
☐ Remodeling	☐ Siding
☐ Roof replacement	☐ Driveway replacement

☐ Pool
☐ Spa
☐ Yard sprinklers
☐ Paneling
☐ Molding
☐ Floodlights
☐ Alarm system
☐ Fireplace
☐ Storage closets
☐ Greenhouse
☐ Solar devices
☐ Stables
☐ Septic tank/sewer
☐ Skylights/windows
☐ Kitchen cabinets
☐ Ceiling fans
☐ Linoleum/tiling
☐ Kitchen counters
☐ Waterproofing
☐ Window treatments (interior)
☐ Theft deterrents
☐ Satellite dish

☐ Tennis court
☐ Barbecue pit
☐ Major landscaping
☐ Central air-conditioning
☐ Added insulation (don't forget the tax credit)
☐ Finish basement
☐ Gutters and downspouts
☐ New water heater
☐ Gazebo
☐ Exhaust fans
☐ Fences
☐ Built-in furniture/shelves
☐ Oil burner
☐ Wall-to-wall carpeting
☐ Bathroom replacements: toilet, sink, tub, shower, bidet
☐ Enclosing terrace or patio
☐ Planters, flower beds
☐ Storm doors, windows
☐ Electronic gating
☐ Home-regulating computer

(Note: Adding the cost of capital improvements to the price you paid for your dwelling may reduce your capital gains.)

As you did on your dwelling evaluation, use a small notebook or separate sheets of paper to note the items to be added or upgraded, the time frame, and the estimated cost. You may want to add a year to the month or season of your time frame.

■ New Home or Vacation Home Purchase

Nearly everybody I know dreams of a new home or a home in the mountains, by the sea, or in the desert. Take a few minutes to reflect on what you would like as features in your dream home. Consider including in your reflection these items:

DREAM A LITTLE DREAM:
No Junk and No Skeletons in Any Closets

Take a few minutes to imagine that a person comes unexpectedly to your home, offering to buy all that you have, even though you hadn't posted any "For Sale" signs. However, she wants to see all that you have before she makes an offer on any portion of it. You will retain the right to sell anything on which she bids.

Imagine that you have just heard this proposition. Once you are over your shock at her proposal, you decide that this may be a blessing—a transaction that could work for your advantage. Which closets or areas of your home would you not want to open to this potential buyer? What would you make available to her? What would you like to sell? What would you buy in its place? How would you feel about being able to unload some of your things? How would you feel about upgrading certain items?

Write freely as thoughts and images come to your mind:

_____

_____

_____

_____

_____

_____

_____

_____

_____

_____

_____

_____

_____

_____

_____

_____

_____

_____

_____

_____

_____

_____

_____

☐ Location
☐ Reasons to move
☐ Number of people living in home
☐ Vacation home(s)
☐ Space requirements
☐ Furnishing needs
☐ Moving costs
☐ Land-use ideas
☐ Energy-saving ideas
☐ Price range

☐ Estimated length of stay in next home
☐ Special needs (such as no stairs, no yard to mow)
☐ Time constraints (or date you hope to move in)
☐ Preliminary data needed to make decisions
☐ Landscaping ideas

Note your ideas about your dream home:

_____

_____

_____

You may even want to sketch a basic plan of the house or look through plan books or magazines to find a plan that appeals to you.

■ Maintenance Checklist for the Home

Beyond repairs, refurbishing, and replacement, most homes require ongoing maintenance. Check the items that pertain to your home, and next to each item, make notes about your maintenance provider, maintenance schedule, or need to establish a maintenance protocol.

	Service and Supplier
☐ Carpet cleaning	
☐ Duct cleaning	
☐ Replacement of filters	
☐ Chimney cleaning	
☐ Trash removal	
☐ Septic service	

	Service and Supplier
☐ Snow removal	
☐ Tennis court maintenance	
☐ Swimming pool maintenance	
☐ Lawn service	
☐ Tree trimming, brush cutting	
☐ Furnace service	
☐ Water heater checkup	
☐ Wood delivery	
☐ Window cleaning	
☐ Cable TV checkup	

■ An Evaluation of Your Vehicles

Just as you have assessed your home(s), you'll want to evaluate each of your vehicles; include automobiles, vans, trucks, bicycles, motorcycles, airplanes, boats, three-wheelers—any device you use for transportation or recreation.

Name each vehicle, and note the items that need repair or replacement, the date of intended repair or replacement, and the estimated cost. Note major and minor repairs as well as general maintenance (apart from fuel). Also list any new vehicles that you intend to purchase in the near future. If no maintenance or repair is needed, note that, too.

Vehicle	Item/Condition	Date	Est. Cost

■ Vehicle Maintenance Schedule

As a driver or operator, you'll want to note several important pieces of information for each vehicle you are authorized to operate. Duplicate this form, and complete one for each vehicle.

Make: _____

Model: _____

Year: _____

Vehicle registration number: _____

Vehicle license tag number: _____

Estimated amount of tag: _____

Vehicle license tag renewal date: _____

Operator license number: _____

Operator license renewal date: _____

Insurance carrier: _____

Insurance renewal date(s): _____

Estimated amount of annual insurance: _____

Security coded: _____

Maintenance provider: _____

    Address: _____

    Phone number: _____

Maintenance schedule: _____

_____

_____

_____

_____

You may also want to note for each vehicle any parking stickers that you need to update periodically or any toll road or turnpike passes that you may need to renew.

■ An Evaluation of Tools and Small Appliances

Anticipate the maintenance that you need on tools and small appliances. Check the items you own:

☐ Lawn mower   ☐ Chain saw
☐ Trimmer, edger   ☐ Vacuum cleaner
☐ Sewing machine   ☐ Small appliances
☐ Pump(s)   ☐ Telephones
☐ Computer and printer ☐ Answering machine/fax
☐ Leaf blower

List the item, its condition, the date you anticipate for repair or replacement, and the estimated cost.

Item	Condition	Date	Est. Cost

■ An Inventory and Evaluation of Furniture, Large Appliances, and Other Valuable Items

A thorough inventory can help you

- identify items that you might contribute to a charity (for tax credit).
- identify items that you might sell.
- plan a schedule for upgrading, updating, or refurbishing items.
- reevaluate your insurance needs.
- provide a detailed account in case of theft.

Consider items in these categories:

☐ Furniture   ☐ Antiques
☐ Camping/sporting gear ☐ Major appliances
☐ Rugs and carpets   ☐ Jewelry
☐ Artwork   ☐ Major landscaping
☐ Workshop equipment   ☐ Electronic equipment
☐ Office equipment   ☐ Hobby items and equipment

Provide as much detail as you need for each item to document it as a possession. If you have a registration number of an appraisal of the item, note that number or where the valuation document has been filed.

Photograph or make a videotape recording of the exterior of your home, the interior of each room (all angles), and all major pieces of furniture. Photograph your yard, including any patio or poolside furnishings or buildings. Label each photo and correlate it to a written description. Also photograph and describe each artifact, antique, collection, or piece of jewelry.

You're likely to need several sheets of paper for your inventory. For each item, note its value (either its purchase price or its present valuation), its condition (whether it needs repair, replacement, refinishing, reupholstery, and so forth), the date by which you think it should be replaced or repaired, and the estimated cost of replacement or repair.

■ Safety Deposit Box Contents

If you have a safety deposit box, you may want to have a record of what is in it—not only as a ready reminder to yourself but as a means of alerting family members to its presence in the event of your death or incapacitating illness. List here the information that is pertinent to your situation. Describe each item, and note the date you stored it.

Safety deposit box location: _____

Number: _____ Location of key: _____

Contact person at location: _____

Item	Description	Date Stored

■ Investment Property

Stocks, bonds, and other financial documents are included in chapter 4. Real property investments, however, may be regarded as material possessions, so they are included here:

☐ Rental property (land, houses, or apartments)

☐ Land (occupied or vacant)

☐ Time-share vacation homes (condominiums, apartments)

☐ Farm or ranch

☐ Commercial real estate

☐ Oil, gas, or mineral rights

☐ Artifacts, rare items, coins, antiquities

You may be part of a pool of owners or investors. The property may be in the United States or overseas. You may need several sheets of paper to record all property you own completely or partially. For each item, provide

- a full legal description.
- valuation at time of purchase and at present.
- location of item (if not part of legal description).
- percentage of ownership you presently hold (and a list of co-owners, other investors, or the bank or lending institution that may hold a mortgage).
- any other details pertaining to your use of or access to the property, liabilities or potential liabilities associated with the property, or your involvement with the property (such as ongoing management).

If you do not own additional property, you may want to make notes related to investment property that you desire to purchase in the future. Include details about location, reasons for purchase, amount you desire to spend, and planned date of purchase.

Investment Property Maintenance

For each piece of rental property that you own, you may want to conduct a thorough evaluation in a way similar to what you have done for your home.

Go back to the lists at the beginning of this chapter and note for each rental property an evaluation of property condition, desired capital improvements, and a maintenance checklist. If the property is furnished, conduct a periodic inventory of the furnishings.

Business Property

Your investment property may be property that is owned by your business (especially in cases of sole proprietorship, limited partnerships, and small corporations). Your ownership of the property may be full or partial. If you have property that falls into this category, you'll also want to refer to the checklists earlier in the chapter. Note a thorough evaluation of the property's condition, desired capital improvements, a maintenance checklist, a complete inventory of furnishings and equipment, and a maintenance checklist for equipment.

If you own vehicles as part of your business, refer to the vehicle checklists and prepare an evaluation of each vehicle's condition and information for each vehicle's maintenance.

Take Time

Take time today . . .
> For flowers, knowing the rosebuds are especially fragrant.
> For birds, knowing there may be fewer robins next spring.
> For children, knowing they too soon fly like arrows from the bow.
> For play, knowing you're never too grown up to benefit from it.
> For older people, knowing that older often means wise.
> For your family, knowing it is the inner circle of life.
> For nature, knowing you can't put it on your charge card.
> For animals, knowing it's their world, too.
> For books, knowing that they are a transport of wisdom that can take you to places you've never imagined.
> For work, knowing that you can't enjoy the view unless you climb the mountain.
> For your health, knowing it's a precious commodity.
> For prayer, knowing it's where you will meet your Lord.

■ Taxation of Your Possessions

In addition to periodic upkeep, your possessions are nearly always subject to some level and degree of taxation. Make notes related to taxation.

Property subject to taxation: _____

    Current assessed value: _____

    Amount of annual taxation: _____

    Taxes remitted to: _____

Property subject to taxation: _____
    Current assessed value: _____
    Amount of annual taxation: _____
    Taxes remitted to: _____

Property subject to taxation: _____
    Current assessed value: _____
    Amount of annual taxation: _____
    Taxes remitted to: _____

Property subject to taxation: _____
    Current assessed value: _____
    Amount of annual taxation: _____
    Taxes remitted to: _____

■ Insurance of Property and Valued Possessions

Virtually all property needs to be insured against fire, natural catastrophe, and theft. No doubt you already have insurance policies that cover your home, vehicle, and personal property. Note here the key aspects of your insurance coverage and the date of the last review session you had with your insurance agent. I've provided one form so that you can duplicate it for several policies. You may want to attach one form as a cover sheet to each policy you presently carry.

Insurance carrier: _____
Policy number: _____
Agent name: _____
    Agent address: _____
    Agent phone number: _____
Policy covers: _____
    Coverage includes: _____
    _____
    Date policy was last reviewed with agent: _____
    Date of renewal: _____
    Amount of annual premium: _____

If your mortgage includes an insurance provision, note the mortgage holder among your insurance carriers.

A growing number of people are insuring themselves for payoff of their credit cards and loans in the event of death or disability. These policies are directly tied to material possessions. Include these policies and the insurance carriers among the policies you have listed.

Key Questions to Ask About Your Insurance Coverage

Do I need this insurance? (Weigh the risks of not having a particular type of insurance. Evaluate each policy you presently hold.) _____

_____

_____

_____

Do I have the right types of insurance? (Have someone list the advantages and disadvantages of a particular financial vehicle for you in clear, readily understood terms.) _____

_____

_____

Are my deductibles too low or too high? (If you are paying premiums for the lowest possible deductible on the highest amount of coverage, the chances are that you will pay out a great deal more than you will ever recover in claims. Use insurance not as a means of covering small accidents or losses but as a means of covering major losses.) _____

_____

_____

_____

Is my coverage adequate? (Your situation may have changed since you purchased a particular policy. What was once right for you may not be right now. Reevaluate at least once every five years; also reevaluate if you have major beneficiary changes [spouse, children] or if a property greatly increases or decreases in value.)

_____

_____

_____

Is everything of value insured? (As you evaluated your insurance coverage, did you find properties or possessions that are not insured?)

_____

_____

_____

■ Putting Things in Order

It isn't enough to know that your possessions have been identified and classified as to their value and state of repair. You face another challenge in putting your stuff into some semblance of easy-to-use, easy-to-store order.

There are various categories for you to consider in sorting, upgrading, and making the best use of your possessions. Consider for each item the need to

- sort into categories.
- label thoroughly (or provide descriptions).
- provide for clean storage.
- keep a written inventory or index of all items.
- purchase containers, dividers, or other devices to enable you to sort and store items suitably.

Things to Sort

Those who seek the LORD shall not lack any good thing.
—Psalm 34:10

Check all of the items that you know you need to sort through and put into order:

- ☐ Books
- ☐ Key reference books
- ☐ Audiocassette tapes
- ☐ Photographs
- ☐ File cabinets
- ☐ Dresser drawers
- ☐ Kitchen cabinets
- ☐ Broom closet
- ☐ Utility closet
- ☐ Desk drawers
- ☐ Coupons
- ☐ Clothes

- ☐ Magazines (issues you want to keep)
- ☐ Videotapes
- ☐ Home movies
- ☐ Clothes closets
- ☐ Pantry
- ☐ Linen closet
- ☐ Workshop
- ☐ Laundry room
- ☐ Boxes in storage
- ☐ Collectibles
- ☐ Shoes

- ☐ Accessories (scarves, ties, bows, belts)
- ☐ Gifts
- ☐ Computer diskettes
- ☐ Packing supplies
- ☐ Gardening tools
- ☐ Scrapbooks/memorabilia
- ☐ Purses

- ☐ Recipes
- ☐ Take-out menus
- ☐ Addresses/phone numbers
- ☐ Office supplies
- ☐ Decorating items (perhaps by season, event, or color scheme)
- ☐ Other: _____

_____

Put an asterisk by any of the categories that you consider to be in urgent need of sorting.

Things to Repair

Include in your list of things to repair items that may need mending, reweaving or redying, altering, professional cleaning, refinishing, restoring, or stain removal. Ask yourself,

- Is it cheaper to buy new than to repair old?
- Will I use this item after I have fixed it?
- How long has it been since I used this item? (If it's been more than a year since you used the item or wore the outfit, chances are, you don't need it or it's out of style. You may be better off to discard it than to spend money on its repair.)
- Do I need professional help? (You may not have the necessary skills to do a thorough or quality job, or it may take you far longer than a professional to do the job.)
- Does this item give me aesthetic pleasure, or do I value it as an heirloom? (Some things are worth fixing or saving in cracked or broken form simply because you like them or because they have meaning to you.)

Item	Who Can Fix	Needed to Fix	Date	Cost

Things to Discard

As you sort your possessions, be on the alert for items that you might throw away, give away, recycle, or sell. If you have an item that warrants throwing away or recycling, don't bother putting it on your list. Throw it away or put it in a bin to take to the recycling center.

Items to Give Away

Items that you might give away need be listed only if you want to keep a running list for use in making a donation of items, substantiating tax records, or storing items for a later sort by charity.

Item to Give Away	To Whom	Deduction Value

Items to Sell

Items that you might sell need be listed only if you want to keep a list as you organize a garage sale or as you sort items for placing them at consignment resale outlets.

Item	When/Where	Asking Price

If you see a garage, estate, or yard sale in your future, can you set a date for that? _____ If you are planning to donate your items to a church or charity sale of some kind, is there a date you can set as a goal? _____

Things to Return

As you sort your possessions, you may find items that belong to others. List items that need to be returned; include items that you know you need to replace (because you have damaged the item). Any item that you have borrowed should be returned clean and in good working order.

Item	To Whom	Notes

Things to Give as Gifts

Here we're talking about gifts you want to give *now*. What would you most like to give to a person? Not simply as a Christmas gift next year but as a major gift of remembrance or as an expression of your deepest love. Tangible gifts include gifts of time or service. Tangible gifts are ultimately things that require the use of money or material substance. What intangible gifts would you like to impart to another person? Intangible gifts are things that you would give to a person if you could—self-esteem, joy, health, love.

As you reflect on both the intangibles and the tangibles in your gift giving, try to relate the two. Are there tangible gifts that evoke the intangible? Is there some way in which you can give the intangible in practical ways?

Person	Tangible Gifts	Intangible Gifts

Things to Upgrade for Use

In this category you may want to consider items to frame (such as photos, artifacts, diplomas, or artwork), items to iron (such as table linens), items to polish (such as silver, copper, brass), and/or items to record (perhaps making master tapes for your system of recordings).

For each item, indicate the work that needs to be done, the person you anticipate will do the work, the date by which you would like to see the item ready for use, and the estimated cost of upgrading (or the maximum amount you are willing to spend).

Item	Work Needed	By Whom	Date	Cost

Designated Spaces

Check the items you store in a specific space. If you do not have a designated space for each of the following items, you may want to assign one!

☐ Keys (each labeled)

☐ Eyeglasses (or contact lenses)

☐ Hearing aid

☐ Dentures

☐ Pocket change

☐ Car registration and proof of insurance (kept in car)

☐ Claim tickets

☐ Medications

☐ Cleaning supplies

☐ Basic office supplies, such as scissors, tape, stapler, ruler, paper clips

☐ Basic home repair tools, such as hammer, pliers, screwdriver

☐ Warranties and registration cards

☐ First aid kit

☐ Yard and garden equipment

☐ Children's toys

☐ Recyclable items

☐ Children's bicycles and other athletic gear

☐ Pieces to uniforms (such as scouting uniforms)

☐ Camping and other outdoor gear

☐ Holiday decorations

☐ Spices

☐ Wrapping paper, ribbon, gift bags, tags

☐ Craft supplies

■ Things to Make

Thus far, you have dealt primarily with identifying and sorting existing items in your possession. But you may be a maker who enjoys creating and giving handcrafted gifts or gifts that flow from your creativity.

Handmade gifts generally cost far more in time than they do in materials. And creative one-of-a-kind gifts—items that flow from one's creativity and cannot be duplicated—are truly priceless.

Here are a few questions you may want to ask about the items you are making:

Is it reasonable to think that I will actually finish this project (or complete a project already started)? _____

How much time can I reasonably give to completion of this project? _____

Will the person for whom I'm making this item be able to wear it or use it by the time I get it completed? _____

Will I need help in finishing this project (such as blocking needlework, backing or framing artwork)? _____

List the items that you plan to make.

Item to Make	Type of Handcraft	Recipient	Date

■ Things to Leave to Others

Most of us have something of a material nature that we hope or intend to leave to others. As you anticipate leaving items or properties to others, the key question to ask yourself is this: Is my will up-to-date?

This presumes, of course, that you have a legal will. If you don't have one, you need one. Otherwise, the final disposition of your material possessions will be left to someone else's decision making.

Your statement of "last will" should include (1) your burial wishes and desires regarding your funeral or memorial service, including your preference of funeral director, (2) a list of relatives, friends, and others to be notified, (3) authorization of donation of your body or organs to medical centers or medical schools if you

desire, and (4) identification of any benefits that you receive and that your benefici-
aries should now receive from the following:

- Union
- Fraternal organization
- Burial society
- Mortgage (especially if you have a paid-up clause at death)
- Life insurance policies
- Health and accident policies
- Workmen's compensation insurance
- Airline insurance policy
- Civil service (if you were employed more than eighteen months)
- Military
- Gas or oil company (royalties)
- Corporation (dividends)
- Publisher (royalties)

It should also (5) list companies, banks, and/or stockbrokers that your survi-
vors should contact, as well as landlords, name of lawyer, name of insurance
companies, and telephone and utility companies (from whom you receive service),
(6) give the name of your accountant or tax preparer (unless an estate lawyer will
prepare the final tax return), (7) list credit cards, charge accounts, subscriptions,
and other accounts that need to be closed, (8) give the location of key documents
(such as safety deposit box information), (9) record personal notes to heirs, and
(10) specify bequests of cash and property.

If you want to leave a particular item or object to a person, you need to state
so in your will—don't just tell a relative or mark the item with the person's name.
No matter how small or insignificant the bequest may be, put it in writing.

If you have not yet made a will, or if you anticipate revising or updating your
will in the near future, you may want to use the lists in the following pages as you
plan the disposition of your estate.

Another document to consider is the living will. Normally, medical professionals use whatever means available to prolong life as long as possible, but the
living will protects your rights should you wish to be treated in a different manner.
A living will form is provided. You can use this form as is, or ask your attorney to
provide you with a form that you can keep on file.

A LIVING WILL

TO MY FAMILY, MY PHYSICIAN, MY LAWYER, MY CLERGYPERSON
TO ANY MEDICAL FACILITY IN WHOSE CARE I HAPPEN TO BE
TO ANY INDIVIDUAL WHO MAY BECOME RESPONSIBLE FOR MY HEALTH, WELFARE,
   OR AFFAIRS:

Death is as much a reality as birth, growth, maturity, and old age—it is the one certainty of
life. If the time comes when I, _____,
can no longer take part in decisions for my own future, let this statement stand as an
expression of my wishes while I am still of sound mind.

If the situation should arise in which there is no reasonable expectation of my recovery
from physical or mental disability, I request that I be allowed to die and not be kept alive
by artificial means or "heroic measures." I do not fear death itself as much as the
indignities of deterioration, dependence, and hopeless pain. I, therefore, ask that
medication be mercifully administered to me to alleviate suffering even though this
may hasten the moment of death.

This request is made after careful consideration. I hope you who care for me will feel
morally bound to follow its mandate. I recognize that this appears to place a heavy
responsibility upon you, but it is with the intention of relieving you of such responsibility
and of placing it upon myself in accordance with my strong convictions that this statement
is made.

Signed _____

Date: _____

Witness: _____

Witness: _____

Copies of this request have been given to:

_____

_____

_____

Disposition of My Body and Organs

_____

_____

_____

Burial Desires and Information

_____

_____

_____

Relatives and Friends to Notify at Time of My Death

_____

_____

_____

Companies and Business Associates to Notify

_____

_____

_____

Accounts to Close at Time of My Death

_____

_____

_____

Location of Key Documents

_____

_____

_____

Notes to Leave to Heirs

_____

_____

_____

Bequests of Money and Property

_____

_____

_____

■ Things to Purchase

Finally, but certainly not least in your management of personal possessions is your "to buy" list. Ask yourself,

- Am I pursuing quality? (Quality items are those that last and have the greatest potential for increasing in value over the years. Quality items are generally durable, repairable, and of classic style and design. They are generally expensive but may not be the most expensive items available for purchase.)
- Is it better to purchase used or new? (Antiques, antiquities, rare collectibles, and many highly valued properties are used—and yet can be of greater value than new comparable items. A used item of high quality may be a better purchase than a new item of lesser quality. On the other hand, a new item may outlast a used item or be more readily repaired. Each item should be evaluated independently.)
- Will I want this item in five years? (Not all items, of course, have a life span of five years. Some items are for immediate consumption; some should last a hundred years.)
- How soon do I need this item? (In this category, want and need are two different things. If you don't need an item immediately, don't go into debt for it! Save for it and purchase it when you can readily afford it.)

You'll probably want to keep a running list of items to purchase, so you may need several sheets of paper. Note the item, the place or person from whom you expect to make the purchase, the price you expect to pay (or amount you have budgeted), and the date you expect to make the purchase. If you don't expect to make the purchase within the next five years, you might want to put "Future." Also note any information you may need to get to make a wise purchase—such as consulting a consumer guide or comparison shopping. You may also want to prioritize purchases for the immediate future.

■ Reflecting On Your Possessions

What you choose to purchase, keep, sell, or possess is up to you. You need to do some soul-searching about the material goods you acquire and your motivations for acquiring them. Ultimately, you need very little in this life to live—enough food and water for today, fresh air to breathe, sufficient clothing for the climate and weather, sufficient housing for a sense of personal safety and comfort, and loved ones with whom to share life's journey. Keep in mind three life principles as you acquire possessions.

Total Security Is a Myth

Seek first the kingdom of God and His righteousness, and all these things shall be added to you.
—Matthew 6:33

Most people envision a successful life as a secure one. Toward that end, they seek to invest in savings plans, IRAs, and insurance. They make their homes secure with locks and elaborate alarm systems. They put their valuables in vaults where they rarely see them.

The truth is that security is never possible with a 100 percent money-back guarantee. Nothing and no one—except God—can assure you of ultimate security. No person has ever lived an entire life totally secure from start to finish.

Life is inherently risky. Whether crossing the street, entering a relationship, starting a company, beginning a new job, or planting a crop, you are taking a risk.

The biggest risk to avoid, however, is the risk of doing nothing. In dealing with your possessions, you must come to grips with this matter of security and risk. Ask yourself,

Am I acquiring things in order to have a greater sense of security in my life?

_____

_____

Am I willing to risk my possessions to gain greater success in the physical, family, spiritual, or mental parts of my life? _____

_____

_____

We Are Only Partially What We Possess

Many people define themselves by their possessions. They are what they own: the house they live in, the car(s) they drive, the clothes and jewelry they wear, the address at which they work, the latest toy that they have purchased. They see themselves as a collection of desirable goods, not as desirable persons with a disposable collection.

Don't look to your possessions as your identity. Let your possessions flow from your inner values and beliefs, your inner desires to create and help others, your inner sense of what is truly worthwhile in life.

The best "possessions" will always be good health, a loving family, peace of mind, new ideas, and a growing spiritual life. To keep possessions in balance, remember this age-old principle: use things and love people.

Ask yourself,

To what extent do I rely on outward appearance to define me and my success to others? _____

_____

_____

If I was stripped of all my possessions, who would I be? _____

_____

_____

Design and Style Require Planning and Management

Your possessions will never take on a distinctive identity or be truly an expression of your individuality unless you plan for their acquisition and manage them wisely.

Design and style take effort. Guard against spur-of-the-moment purchases, shoddy substitutes, and the latest fads. Search out the best of what you like, and go for the highest quality in what you need.

Some people ask, "Is it acceptable for a Christian to be concerned with style?" I don't see how you can avoid establishing a style for yourself. Your choices are individual. The development of your personal style is ultimately a manifestation of the principle "To thine own self be true." Finding and being true to your style take sincere soul-searching and ongoing discipline.

You were created by God as a unique and distinctive individual. You have tastes, abilities, and desires that no one else has. You have distinctive likes and dislikes. The Lord made you with free will, with the ability to choose. You are called to a unique purpose in life, and you are given unique opportunities and challenges.

Much of what is called stewardship in the church is a matter of managing the goods that come into your possession. What you do with your money is ultimately a reflection of who you are and the choices you make out of your unique being. To whom you give or with whom you share possessions is a reflection of your spiritual nature—it is an act of worship to God and an act of love of others (both of which fulfill the commandments given by Jesus Christ).

You are called to give with thought, care, and deliberation. You are not to be swayed by the messages of the world at large but to be driven by your convictions as to what the Lord would desire and find pleasing for you to do and to give.

Give and buy and sell with care. Make your possessions a reflection of what you value and what you believe. And then use your possessions to further what you value and what you believe. You'll experience greater harmony in your life.

Ask yourself,

What is my style? _____

_____

_____

What motivates me to buy, sell, or give? _____

_____

_____

What is worthy of my possession? _____

_____

_____

Are my possessions a reflection of what I believe about myself and about God?

_____

_____

Am I using my possessions as an act of worship to God and to further His kingdom on this earth?_____

_____

_____

What of my material goods am I willing to give? _____

_____

_____

■ Summing Up and Setting Goals

We have a mixed-bag relationship to things. When stripped of everything, we feel the weight of worry. When laden with too much, we feel the weight of stress.

As you reflect on this chapter, try to sum up your feelings and opinions about material goods. In particular, look for ways in which you have

- indicated a desire to eliminate things from your life.
- indicated a desire to acquire things.
- indicated a desire to trade in things or upgrade things.
- indicated a desire to use things in a new way.

Summary Statements

Write in one paragraph or less the degree to which you are comfortable with your current possessions. If you are uncomfortable with them, why and in what ways?

_____

_____

_____

_____

How much responsibility do you feel for your things? Describe that responsibility.

_____

_____

_____

_____

As you look back through this chapter, what recurring thought do you have?

_____

_____

_____

_____

_____

If you had to write just one word or phrase to motivate yourself toward better management of your material possessions, what would that word or phrase likely be? _____

Goal Statements

Take another look through this chapter, and write as many goal statements as come to your mind related to your possessions.

Examples of ineffective and effective possessions-related goal statements are given below:

Ineffective:
Organize my life.
Make a will.

Effective:
I will clean out one closet each Saturday for the next eight weeks.
I will make an appointment with an attorney tomorrow morning.

Your goals related to your possessions may be short-range, mid-range, or long-range. Some of your goals in this section may involve other people. Note goals that you may not be able to do by yourself.

My Goals Related to My Material Goods

Write your goals for improved management of your possessions.

_____
_____
_____
_____
_____
_____
_____
_____
_____
_____
_____
_____

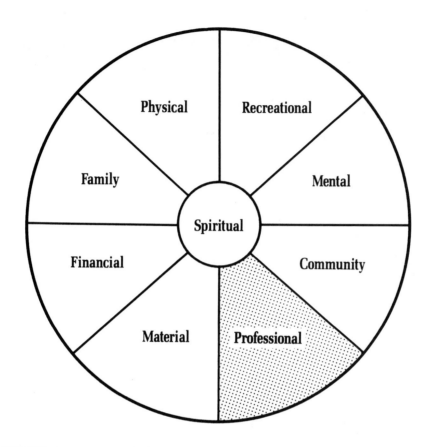

SECRET: Pursue your mission, not your pension.

SCRIPTURE: "Better is a little with righteousness, than vast revenues without justice" (Prov. 16:8).

6

Making the Most of
Your God-Given Abilities

YOU ARE a talented person—whether you think so or not. Every person has at least one talent, something he or she can do well. In giving your talent away—using it, performing it, helping others with it, exercising it—you will see that talent bless others, and it will increase and bring reward back to you.

Jesus taught this in a very direct way in His parables on giving and on the investment of talents. (See Matt. 25:15–30 and Luke 19:12–27.) No matter how much was given to each of the people in the stories, those who used or invested what was given to them *doubled* their return, and they earned the praise and honor of their master.

Ideally, your career—your job, your profession, your work—reflects your abilities, and it is your opportunity to use the unique gifts that God has given you. In some cases, however, people operate, as it were, outside their talents. They are in careers for which they are not innately qualified, in which they are disinterested, or for which they have no aptitude. As a result, they are usually miserable or feel tremendous stress.

I have known that kind of stress. After high school, I went to the U.S. Naval Academy at Annapolis where strong emphasis was put on marine engineering, electrical engineering, navigation, ordnance, and gunnery. I struggled through those studies and went on to flight school where I struggled further with subjects for which I wasn't naturally gifted. As a carrier-based attack pilot, I held my own due mostly to quick reflexes, determination, and an excellent memory. Flying supersonic navy jets, however, was not my natural gift. I was operating outside my talents. Had I understood my natural gifts as a teenager, I would have discovered

DREAM A LITTLE DREAM:
Your Ultimate Workbench

Take a few minutes to imagine that you have just received a diploma that is also a free ticket to your dream job. You simply need to turn in your ticket and receive your ultimate workbench: the place and job and associates that you desire.

Walk into the work space you choose. What is the work that you will do in that space? Who are your coworkers? What are they doing? Describe your work environment. What does it look like, feel like, smell like, sound like? How do you feel in this setting? What do people say to you, ask of you, or report to you? What rewards do you experience?

Write freely as thoughts and images come to your mind:

_____

_____

_____

_____

_____

_____

_____

_____

_____

_____

_____

_____

_____

_____

_____

_____

_____

_____

_____

_____

_____

_____

_____

_____

_____

that the more appropriate course for my life would have been to go to a university to pursue studies in English, foreign language, music, the fine arts, writing, and speaking—which would have yielded information and helped me develop the very skills I use and enjoy using today.

You need to ask two main questions as you approach these exercises and reflections related to your professional life:

1. Is my current professional career the one best suited to me? (If it is not, you need to begin planning immediately to get into an area that gives you an opportunity to best express and explore the abilities God has given you.)
2. If I am in the best career suited to me, am I using my talents to their maximum? (That question is very often related to your current employment and the job description you fill. It is also related to your motivational level, your affiliations, the degree to which you have developed your talents, and your professional aspirations.)

You'll explore possible answers to each question in this chapter.

■ Identifying Your Unique Aptitudes

Your talents—which also may be stated as aptitudes—are very specific psychological and physiological tendencies. They are rooted in your natural being and, to a great extent, may very well be part of your genetic makeup.

Certain people, for example, have an enhanced ability to hear and differentiate sounds. Others have greater physical coordination—small motor skills, large muscle skills, eye-hand coordination, and so forth. Some people seem intuitively to see logical connections where others see nothing or to understand mechanical devices that leave others clueless.

The only way you can truly know *all* of your aptitudes is to take a quality aptitude test.

Ask yourself,

Why am I doing what I do? (Did a parent or grandparent encourage you to pursue that field? Did a teacher encourage you? Did you find that you liked the field you're in well enough to do what it took to succeed in it, or did it come easy for you?) _____

_____

If I had it to do over, what career do I think I would pursue? (Would you have taken a different course of study in college? What would you have tried as an elective?)

_____

_____

If I knew there was absolutely no way I could fail at it, what would I like to pursue, be, or do as a profession? _____

_____

_____

What did I dream of doing when I was a child? _____

_____

_____

What is it that I can't NOT do? (In other words, do you love to write so much that you'd have to write even if nobody ever paid you for anything you had written? Do you love to tinker with things that even if you didn't have a job in that area, you'd have to be building something or tearing something apart to see how it works or how it might work better?)

_____

_____

Have I taken a genuine aptitude test? (An aptitude test is not a career orientation test or a psychological test. It is a test that truly measures aptitudes. An aptitude test that I value highly is the one used by the Johnson O'Connor Research Foundation. [It has its headquarters in New York, but there are Human Engineering Laboratories in major cities across the nation.]

A growing number of aptitude tests are available in bookstores for self-administration. Although these aren't likely to be as reliable or as thorough as tests that check your skills objectively [all self-administered tests are, by their very nature, subjective analyses], they may give you clues as to which areas you should explore further. Some of these tests now link personality traits to careers.)

_____

_____

If you have not taken an aptitude test, I heartily recommend that you do so. You may want to state that as a goal.

Aptitudes

Only after attempting to persuade you to take a thorough, objective aptitude test am I willing to share with you the nineteen aptitudes that are tested by the Johnson O'Connor Research Foundation Laboratories. Remember that your appraisal of your own abilities, with regard to this list, is a *subjective* response. Still, it may give you a starting point as you explore more fully your unique talents and abilities.

Check off the areas in which you believe you would score highly. (Few people score high in more than five areas.)

☐ Personality—
    ☐ Objective, suited best for working with others
    ☐ Subjective, suited more for specialized, individual work
☐ Graphoria—clerical ability in dealing with figures and symbols
☐ Ideaphoria—creative imagination or expression of ideas
☐ Structural visualization—ability to visualize solids and think in three dimensions
☐ Inductive reasoning—ability to form logical conclusions from fragmented facts
☐ Analytical reasoning—ability to resolve an idea into its component parts
☐ Finger dexterity—ability to manipulate fingers skillfully
☐ Tweezer dexterity—ability to handle small tools with precision
☐ Observation—ability to take careful notice
☐ Design memory—ability to remember designs easily
☐ Tonal memory—ability to remember sounds and express an ear for music
☐ Pitch discrimination—ability to differentiate musical tones
☐ Rhythmic ability—ability to maintain a set rhythmic timing

☐ Timbre discrimination—ability to distinguish sounds of the same pitch and volume from each other

☐ Number memory—ability to store many things in your mind at the same time

☐ Proportional appraisal—ability to distinguish relative and harmonious proportions

☐ Silograms—ability to learn unfamiliar words and languages

☐ Foresight—ability to look ahead prudently

☐ Color perception—ability to distinguish colors

As you reflect on the areas you've marked, ask yourself these questions:

Does my current job call on me to use these abilities routinely? _____
Does my current job expect me to use abilities that I do not believe are among my aptitudes? _____

Professional Fields and Skills

As much as I advocate early aptitude testing, I also see value in other types of psychological and career-oriented testing to help people focus on the type of work they will find most rewarding in life, and in which they might enjoy the greatest personal achievement and satisfaction.

A more generalized career-planning test is useful primarily in pointing a person toward either a professional field or a professional skill. Let me briefly describe the difference.

A *professional field* includes a number of jobs focused on a particular service or body of information. An example of a professional field might be health care. Within the field of health care are many different jobs, each of which requires certain specialized aptitudes. The work of a nurse is vastly different from that of a neurosurgeon, a pathologist, or a teacher in a medical school.

A *professional skill* is an ability to do something, which may be applied to any number of subject areas. An example of a professional skill may be the ability to discriminate among features or the ability to verbalize ideas quickly and fluently. A combination of these two skills may well point a person toward sales. But what to sell? Cars or herbicides? Insurance or clothing? Hardware or software?

Answer these questions related to professional fields and skills:

What professional fields do I find interesting? (You may list the field in which you are currently working, but extend your thinking to several other fields that are intriguing to you. List at least five fields.)

1. _____
2. _____
3. _____
4. _____
5. _____

What professional skills do I believe I have? (A partial list is given below. Check off skills that you believe apply to you. Cross through ones that are definitely not you. You'll see some duplication here with the aptitudes provided on previous pages. The skills here are to be checked off only if you have good reason to believe that you currently use them or have used them in work you have done. The skill may be one you have developed through years of education and experience, even if it isn't necessarily a basic aptitude. Go beyond this list to note any other skills that you believe are among your abilities.)

☐ Spatial design
☐ Musical ability
☐ Ability to express self in artistic ways
☐ Ability to analyze data for patterns
☐ Ability to put things in sequential order
☐ Good small motor skills
☐ Good large muscle coordination
☐ Ability to read and comprehend
☐ Ability to remember visual information (e.g., faces)
☐ Physical stamina
☐ Ability to stay in control in crises
☐ Enjoy being with people
☐ High motivation to complete tasks

☐ Logical abilities
☐ Ability to differentiate colors
☐ Ability to manipulate numbers
☐ Ability to listen and recall information given orally
☐ Ability to remember message of written material
☐ Ability to concentrate for long periods of time
☐ Physical strength
☐ Ability to recall experience
☐ Ability to differentiate between shapes and sizes
☐ Prefer working alone
☐ Intuitive understanding of people's motives
☐ Enjoy argument

☐ Like to deal only with facts
☐ Good problem-solving skills
☐ Ability to draw
☐ High sense of order
☐ Enjoy research
☐ Enjoy puzzles
☐ Ability to follow instructions
☐ Good with detail
☐ Self-starter
☐ Generally good foresight
☐ High creativity
☐ Ability to take apart an argument
☐ Sound differentiation
☐ Ability to communicate verbally (orally)
☐ Ability to communicate in writing
☐ Ability to note differences and similarities

☐ Enjoy expression of opinion
☐ Good decision-making skills
☐ Deal well under pressure of deadlines or time
☐ Make decisions quickly
☐ Highly self-motivated to complete tasks
☐ Enjoy precision
☐ Good eye-hand coordination
☐ Ability to visualize
☐ Highly ambitious
☐ Ability to note trends
☐ Ability to plan ahead
☐ Ability to break down large job into smaller tasks
☐ Ability to see proportion
☐ Other: _____
_____
_____

As you reflect on the professional skills you've noted, answer these questions:

What parts of your current job do you do best? _____
_____
_____
_____

What aspects of your current job do you like best? _____
_____
_____
_____

Do you have significant professional skills that are not being used in your present job? _____
_____
_____

Are there aspects of your present job that are highly irritating? _____

_____

_____

What skills required by your job do you need to enhance? _____

_____

_____

Go back and reflect on the professional skills you have claimed as your own. Highlight ones that you feel are directly related to your aptitudes (as opposed to skills you have acquired through arduous work or years of practice).

Right or Left Brain?

Part of your aptitude has to do with the way you think. The research conducted by Dr. Roger Sperry in split-brain experiments led scientists to characterize thinking in two general ways:

Left Hemisphere	Right Hemisphere
(Controls the right side of the body)	(Controls the left side of the body)
Verbal	Nonverbal
Logical	Gestalt
Analytical	Intuitive
Sequential	Spontaneous
Facts	Feelings
Language, math	Art, music
Linear	Spatial
Think in words	Think in visuals
Temporal	Holistic

With which list of words are you more comfortable? _____

Scientists today believe that the brain is not nearly so compartmentalized and that one side of the brain (if damaged, for example) can compensate for the other. Still, in appraising your career path, it may be helpful for you to see these words clustered together.

Be strong and of good courage, do not fear nor be afraid of them; for the LORD your God, He is the One who goes with you. He will not leave you nor forsake you.
—Deuteronomy 31:6

Is your present job one that you would also characterize with the same brain-hemisphere label you give yourself? _____

True Dreams Rarely Die

A genuine heartfelt dream rarely dies. It only goes underground—buried deep within the recesses of your mind—where it often smolders into deep disappointment, resentment, and/or frustration and may erupt at some point as a volcano of violent anger or cause a cave-in of heavy depression.

Furthermore, most dreams shouldn't die. Dreams are rarely ones of destruction, violence, harm, or loss. Most dreams are ones in which we envision a better future, a happier day-to-day life, more fulfilling work, more fulfilling relationships, and deeper, lasting joy. Most dreams are ones in which health, optimism, laughter, friends and close relationships, a feeling of satisfaction, and hope abound—and fear, worry, and stress are nowhere to be found. Most dreams are worth the dreaming!

—Timing Is Everything

■ Maximizing Your Abilities

Achieving your maximum potential requires a number of things: focus, persistence, achievable goals, ability to motivate yourself, ability to evaluate external trends, the right mentors, and in some cases, simply being at the right place at the right time.

Performance Standards

In beginning the planning process for greater professional success, you need to take a look at your past and present work performance, and the standards by which your performance has been evaluated or rewarded.

A Work Resume

Job applications and resumes usually ask for somewhat different information from what is asked of you below. This resume zeroes in on your education, work history, skills training, and certain aspects of your professional career thus far.

Education. Beginning with high school, note each institution or training program you have attended, including seminars or individual courses that were directly aimed at training and had some type of curriculum or educational objectives. Also list any private tutoring or private lessons you have had, whether or not it has been directly related to your career. (Do not include attendance at conventions, professional conferences, one-to-three-day lecture series, and so forth.)

Institution	Course of Study	Degree	Dates

Work experience. Begin with your first full-time job and note all work experiences after that time. (Some experiences may have been part-time or transitional. Do *not* include part-time jobs or work-study grants that you may have had while you were in high school or college. *Do* include all full-time summer jobs and any research projects that were related to your professional growth or development.)

Employer and Area of Company	Job Title and Type of Work	Salary: Start and Final	Dates of Employ	Reason for Leaving

Special skills or training. Note any machines that you are adept at using, any computer languages that you speak, any foreign languages in which you are fluent, any specialized courses you have taken to acquire specific skills or information, and any other instruments, devices, or methods in which you are trained.

Special Skills	Proficiency Level

Professional memberships. List all of the professional organizations or societies to which you have belonged or do belong.

Organization	Brief Description	Dates of Membership

Contributions to your profession. Note any journal articles or books that you have written, any conferences to which you have spoken or submitted papers, any major discoveries you have made, and so forth.

Contribution	Brief Description	Date

Recognition within profession (honors and awards given). Note any awards or honors that have been directly related to your achievement, beginning with major high-school or teen awards.

Honor	Given By	For What	Date

Key associates and mentors. Note the foremost people in your profession with whom you have worked or cowritten articles or books, or under whom you have studied.

Person	Context of Association	Date

As you reflect on what you have prepared as a work resume, ask yourself,

Have I been focused? Is there an overall direction in my professional career or work life? _____

_____

Do I have enough skills to move forward in my career? Are additional skills necessary, or degrees necessary, for me to advance further? Is there a particular area of training that I need to have to keep my current job? _____

_____

You may want to go back through this exercise and make some notes as to how you would like for these forms to read five years from now.

Your Present Job

What is your present job description? Write it here as fully as you can:

_____

_____

_____

_____

Reflect on the job description you have written. Answer these questions:

Is this your understanding of your job, or is this what has been given to you by a supervisor? _____

Is this job description on file with your company in *writing*? _____

Does this job description accurately reflect what you do? If not, what's missing, or what is listed that you don't do? _____

Is there a level of acceptable performance or a system of rewards that is directly related to your job description? _____

Do you have the authority to carry out all of the responsibilities listed here? ____

Has this job description changed in the last year? Has the change been noted by all concerned? Have you been accurately compensated for any increase in your responsibilities? _____

Are you self-employed or the head of a company you founded? Write a job description for yourself anyway. Most of these questions apply to your situation, too.

Performance Evaluation

What is the form or process by which you are evaluated (for continued employment, promotion, or reward)? State it as fully, yet succinctly, as you can.

_____

_____

_____

_____

Reflect on the evaluation method you have written. Ask yourself these questions related to your current level of job performance:

How often is my performance reviewed? _____

As the result of my last performance evaluation, what areas of strength were noted?
_____
_____

What steps am I taking or might I take to build on these strengths? _____
_____

At my last performance review, what areas of weakness were noted?
_____
_____

What steps am I taking or might I take to overcome these weaknesses?
_____
_____

What other suggestions did my evaluating supervisor give me?
_____
_____

How do I feel about my supervisor's suggestions? _____
_____

What does my supervisor envision as my potential within the company (next move upward, next raise in salary, next main opportunity to prove my worth to supervisors)? _____
_____

Are there individuals who may be blocking, intentionally or unintentionally, my success and accomplishments? (Name them and create a way to share your feelings with them.) _____
_____

Do I have mentors or strong supporters within this company?

_____

_____

How high do I believe I can go in this company, given the current state of the company, my job performance, and my associations within the company?

_____

_____

An Overview of the Situation

As you look back at your work record, job description, and current performance, what stands out to you?

Are you succeeding? _____

Are you moving forward in your professional life as rapidly as you would like? _____

Are you satisfied with your level of performance? _____

Do you foresee staying where you are for a while? _____

Do you anticipate a move upward in the near future that may entail a learning curve or a new level of stress related to responsibility? _____

Do you expect to retire from this company? (If so, have you given thought as to what level within the company you expect to achieve by the time you retire?) _____

Is there a chance this company will let you go (due to changes in the company, poor overall company performance, office politics, or your level of performance)? If so, what might you do to change that situation or begin to prepare for a change of employment? _____

_____

_____

Enhancing Your Professional Profile

List five things that you can do—beginning immediately—to enhance your professional profile. Note along with your ideas whether other people are required and in what capacity. Note any obstacles you may have to overcome to enact your ideas.

1. _____
   _____

2. _____
   _____

3. _____
   _____

4. _____
   _____

5. _____
   _____

Staying Current

A big part of any profession is staying current with new information, theories, and procedures. Consider several ways of staying up-to-date or enhancing your understanding of your profession.

Seminars and Conferences

List the conferences, conventions, or seminars you plan to attend in the next five years that are directly related to your profession.

Seminar/ Conference	Sponsoring Organization	Place	Date

Periodicals

List the professional journals to which you presently subscribe. Note along with periodicity whether you read each issue regularly and thoroughly or just pick out occasional articles to read.

Journal or Magazine	Publishing or Sponsoring Organization	Periodicity/ Reading Habit

Now go back to your list and add any journals that you believe might be helpful for you to read. Note under the periodicity column when you expect to subscribe.

Key Books

List at least ten books that you believe would hold valuable professional information for you. They don't necessarily need to be factual or theoretical. They may be books about how to work in a practical way in your profession, biographies or autobiographies about key people in your profession (historical or current), or motivational books that can help you stay focused on, interested in, or enthused about your work life as a whole.

	Book	Author	Content/Gain	Date
1.				
2.				
3.				
4.				
5.				
6.				
7.				
8.				
9.				
10.				

You probably have several reference books in mind to add to your professional library. List at least ten such books.

Reference Book	Publisher/ Company	Content	Date
1.			
2.			
3.			
4.			
5.			
6.			
7.			
8.			
9.			
10.			

Most busy people have to make time to read. Tape sets work well for some people because they can listen in their cars while they drive to and from work or listen with headsets as they commute by train or bus. Other people need to block off a part of their workday to read. Identify the best time and place for you to read or listen to profession-related material.

Best reading time: _____

Best reading place: _____

Networking

Apart from your attendance at conferences, you need to be in association with others in your profession who can challenge you to think about, explore, conduct research in, create, or otherwise produce in an area that you may not have pursued. Networking with both colleagues and mentors is vital for professional growth.

Identify your present colleagues, the area of your profession that is common to you both, and the way in which you have worked, are working, or might work together. Your colleagues may be people within your company or those outside your company with whom you have an ongoing relationship.

Colleague	Professional Area of Mutual Interest	Working Relationship

Reflect on your list. Are there colleagues within your profession that you wish you had? Create a new list with their names. What project might you propose to each person as a collaboration? Note next to each proposed collaboration whether there are any potential conflicts in the two of you working together (for example, the person might work for a competitor or you might speak different languages).

Potential Colleague	Professional Area of Mutual Interest	Possible Collaboration

Teachers and Mentors

Teachers and mentors are similar. Teachers generally evaluate performance and follow a systematic approach in conveying information. Mentors are more likely to be people with whom you have a relationship—formal or informal—and the information they convey is more likely to be practical, encompass the broad spectrum of your professional life (not only your specific job or a specific arena of information), and be ongoing. One person stated the difference this way: "Teachers lecture and grade; mentors converse and answer questions." You need both teachers and mentors as you grow in your professional career.

Teachers

List at least five people in your profession from whom you believe you could learn a great deal.

Teacher	Information to Be Gained	Learning Opportunity	Date
1.			
2.			
3.			
4.			
5.			

Mentors

Think of people from whom you could learn about the practical workings of your profession, your current company, or the new skill that you are attempting to acquire. Who is willing to take you under his or her wing? A good mentor should not be threatened by your success but should applaud it.

Attempt to identify at least three mentors. They may represent different aspects of your professional life. A mentor is a person with whom you should have somewhat frequent and direct contact, and with whom you can spend sufficient time in free-flowing conversation about professional matters.

Mentor	Professional Area	Periodicity of Contact
1.		
2.		
3.		

If these people are not presently your mentors (in a way in which you both recognize that the relationship involves mentoring), you may want to ask the person very directly whether he or she will mentor you in a particular area.

Admired Persons

I keep an ongoing list of persons I admire. I try to hear these people every time I can, and I try to spend time with them as often as I can. They are people I admire for the totality of their lives, including the way they conduct themselves as professionals in their chosen fields. They are not people who do what I do (for the most part), but they are people who have succeeded in their careers and who bear inner qualities that I hope to emulate in my life.

Who do you admire? List at least ten people.

	Person I Admire	Reasons for My Admiration	Our Relationship
1.			
2.			
3.			
4.			
5.			
6.			
7.			
8.			
9.			
10.			

An Inner Motivation to Be Successful

A very large part of what will determine your ability to maximize your potential is your degree of inner motivation. Other words to describe this highly personal motivation might be *ambition* or *drive*.

For many people, the drive to succeed is entirely contained within self. Other people need rivals or competitors to motivate them toward excellence.

Some people need to have fans or cheerleaders before they give their best effort. Others are motivated by rewards.

My Personal Motivational Level

The statements below will give you some indication about your inner motivation to reach your professional potential. Mark your point of agreement along each continuum.

	Disagree	Agree
I try to do my very best no matter what the task or activity.	—┼┼┼┼	┼┼┼┼—
I am a self-starter.	—┼┼┼┼	┼┼┼┼—
Once I've started a task, I can rarely be pulled off track or distracted.	—┼┼┼┼	┼┼┼┼—
I have a great need to complete projects once I've started them.	—┼┼┼┼	┼┼┼┼—
I tend to work even if people around me are goofing off.	—┼┼┼┼	┼┼┼┼—
I value work and task completion very highly.	—┼┼┼┼	┼┼┼┼—
I don't need others to provide constant encouragement, although I find encouragement gratifying.	—┼┼┼┼	┼┼┼┼—
The foremost person against whom I compete is myself.	—┼┼┼┼	┼┼┼┼—
I usually set rewards for myself, not relying on others to recognize my achievement or value.	—┼┼┼┼	┼┼┼┼—

Strong agreement with these statements indicates a high degree of motivation. Reflect on your motivational profile. Answer these questions:

Am I comfortable with my present motivational level? _____

Am I a perfectionist to the point of not completing tasks? _____

Am I motivated to succeed in some aspects of my professional life and not in others? _____

If I need competitors to stay motivated, where do I find them? _____

_____

If I need fans or cheerleaders to stay motivated, where do I find them? _____

_____

Understanding My Motivational Level

What motivates you? Below are some motivators. Check off ones that you believe apply in some way to you. Mark a line through those that you don't believe apply at all.

You need to be concerned primarily with your professional life in marking this list. In other words, mark items in response to the question: What is part of my motivation to succeed in my present job or career?

- ☐ Past poverty, shame, infamy, or failure
- ☐ Need to support or help others in need
- ☐ Desire for money
- ☐ Applause
- ☐ Association with highly motivated people
- ☐ Fear of failure
- ☐ Desire to overcome poor self-esteem
- ☐ Desire to maintain high self-worth
- ☐ Recent reward or award received
- ☐ Need to win (competitive drive)
- ☐ Criticism from others
- ☐ Praise from others
- ☐ Desire for recognition
- ☐ Desire for power
- ☐ Sense of divine purpose
- ☐ Warm feelings, touching
- ☐ Encouraging words, praise
- ☐ Desire to please (God or other people)
- ☐ Fear of punishment
- ☐ Expressions of value and love
- ☐ Desire to be included in group
- ☐ Lack of rewards
- ☐ Dare of colleague
- ☐ Desire to outperform competitor
- ☐ Other: _____

_____

Reflect on the motivations you have noted. Now list at least four rewards that are satisfying to you in response to good work effort or professional success. A reward might be a memo of thanks, a trophy, a raise, a bonus, or any number of tangible or intangible expressions of honor.

Professional rewards I most enjoy receiving:

1. _____
2. _____
3. _____
4. _____

Reflect on this list. When was the last time that you received each of these types of rewards? Put a date next to each award category.

If you aren't being rewarded with some degree of regularity, or if you don't remember the last time you received an award or recognition, ask yourself these questions:

What is keeping me from the rewards that I deserve (and that give me a sense of professional satisfaction and accomplishment)? _____

What might I do to put myself into a position to receive more rewards or a reward long overdue? _____

Who is the reward giver that I value the most? _____

A Greater Sense of Self-Esteem

Some people lack motivation because they don't see themselves as capable or worthy of reaching greater heights. These people generally lack self-esteem. As honestly as you can, answer these questions:

Do you believe you are worthy of success? _____

Do you believe you deserve to be more successful than you are today? _____

Do you believe that there is something in your background or makeup that inherently keeps you from success? _____

Do you believe you are capable of overcoming any weaknesses or faults you have in your quest for greater wholeness? _____

Reflect on your answers. Ask further,

Who is responsible for the level of self-esteem you have today? (Who has told you at some time, in some place, about your worth? To what voice are you listening?) _____

No person can ever fully tell you the truth about yourself because no other person is capable of seeing the full breadth and depth of your life.

Commit to memory these two quotes of the apostle Paul:

I can do all things through Christ who strengthens me (Phil. 4:13).

My God shall supply all your need according to His riches in glory by Christ Jesus (Phil. 4:19).

Paul said *all* things could be done and *all* need could be met in Christ and through Christ. Whatever aspects of your self-esteem are weak or damaged, Christ came to heal and restore! He desires for you truly to be made whole.

Big-Enough Goals

A lack of motivation is sometimes directly linked to the fact that people have lost sight of the big picture—they no longer have a sense of their personal potential or of greater goals they might set for themselves.

Do you need to set some new goals for yourself? If so, identify several of them.

Goal	Way to Begin Achieving It

A God-Given Destiny

Do you have a strong understanding of your purpose on this earth from God's vantage point? Do you have a sense that what you are doing in your professional life is actually an opportunity that the Lord has given to you? Nothing is more motivating than having a keen sense of your God-given destiny.

Reflect for a few minutes about the possibility that your professional life can be an opportunity for ministry and for sharing God's love with others.

_____

_____

_____

_____

Occasionally, a person will say to me, "I realize that I'm doing something as a profession that the Lord *doesn't* want me to do." On rare occasions, the person is involved in a profession that he or she truly believes is displeasing to the Lord. If that is your situation, you need to plan a change in your life's work. You will continually feel torn and under stress if you try to achieve excellence in a profession that you believe is dishonorable to the Lord.

The more common response is for a person to say, "I never thought about my job or my profession as being a God-given opportunity or call." Reflect on that possibility.

Time Is a Terrible Thing to Waste

R. Alec MacKenzie has listed fifteen time wasters. Consider the possibility that these habits or practices are robbing *you* of valuable time as you pursue your professional goals.

1. Telephone interruptions
2. Visitors dropping in without appointments
3. Meetings—both scheduled and unscheduled
4. Crisis situations for which no plans were possible
5. Lack of objectives, priorities, and deadlines
6. Personal disorganization
7. Involvement in routine and detail that should be delegated
8. Attempting too much at once and underestimating the time required
9. Failure to set up clear lines of responsibility
10. Inadequate, inaccurate, or delayed information from others
11. Indecision and procrastination
12. Lack of clear communication or adequate instructions
13. Inability to say no
14. Lack of standards and progress reports that allow you to keep track of developments
15. Fatigue

What might you do to keep these habits or states from wasting your time?

Time, like a snowflake, disappears while you're trying to decide what to do about it.

—*Goal Mining* manual
by Denis Waitley

My Work as My Mission

List at least four ways in which you can see that your current area of work provides an opportunity to express your faith in tangible and practical ways or gives you an opportunity to show God's love to others.

1. _____
2. _____
3. _____
4. _____

■ Summing Up and Setting Goals

We live in a culture in which virtually the first two questions we ask of any stranger are these: "What is your name?" and "What do you do?" Our work defines us—whether we desire to be defined by it or not.

As I read the Scriptures, I find few ignoble or unworthy professions. On the other hand, I see a great many people who were very diligent about their work. The Bible has highly positive things to say about the value of work. We are admonished to pursue the work of our *own* hands, to deal honestly with others in our work-related transactions, to perform our work as a living sacrifice of obedience to the Lord, and not to be lazy. Every person is expected to work to the best of his or her ability.

One of the most important questions you can ever ask yourself is, What did God make me to do? Each person on this earth was created as a unique creature, set in a unique time and place in history, surrounded by unique circumstances and other people, and called to fulfill a unique role. Finding your purpose in life is very closely related to finding your true calling—in other words, your profession.

Our work is, indeed, the way we profess the Lord. It is the way we express His handiwork—ourselves! It is the way we profess His goodness, His creativity, and His love.

As you look back through what you have written in this chapter, certain strengths and weaknesses are likely to stand out to you. Look particularly for

- things you intend to do related to your profession, especially those things next to which you have placed dates.
- ways in which you desire to grow in your abilities.
- any expressed need to better understand your uniqueness.

Summary Statements

In a paragraph or less, write what you perceive to be your true profession.

_____

_____

_____

_____

Write in a paragraph or less a response to the statements that follow: *You cannot succeed in a profession totally by yourself. You depend to a certain degree on others.*

_____

_____

_____

_____

What about your professional life are you looking forward to quitting when you retire? _____

_____

_____

_____

Reflect on what you have just written. If there are things you desire to give up later, why not give them up now? What reasons do you have for continuing to do what you don't find fulfilling or enjoyable? Are those reasons entirely valid? What would happen if you did give up those things now? _____

_____

_____

_____

_____

As you look back through this chapter, what recurring themes or thoughts do you have? _____

_____

_____

_____

What one word or phrase would you use to motivate yourself to new professional heights? _____

Goal Statements

Reread what you have written in your summary statements. Thumb through this chapter one more time. Then write as many goal statements as you desire related to your professional life.

Examples of ineffective/vague and effective/specific profession-related goal statements are given below:

Ineffective:
Get a raise.
Make better use of my talents.

Effective:
I will ask my supervisor tomorrow morning what I need to do to earn a raise in my salary.
I will locate and take an aptitude test within sixty days.

Your goals related to your career may be short-range, mid-range, or long-range. Most of the goals should be things that you can do by yourself for yourself. Note any that require others and ask yourself, What can I do to convince this person to help me achieve my professional goals?

My Professional Goals

Write your goals for enhancing your career.

_____
_____
_____
_____
_____
_____
_____
_____
_____

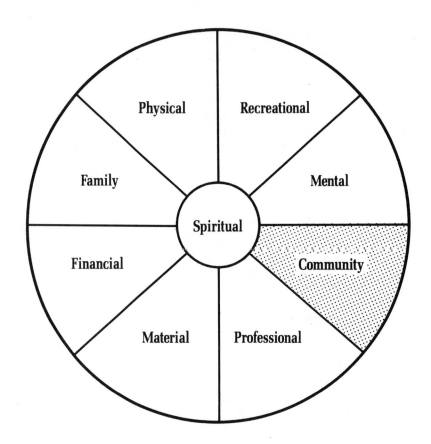

SECRET: True success is measured in the amount of service rendered.

SCRIPTURES: "Inasmuch as you did it to one of the least of these My brethren, you did it to Me" (Matt. 25:40).

"Let your light so shine before men, that they may see your good works and glorify your Father in heaven" (Matt. 5:16).

Serving Your Neighbors

WHO IS my neighbor?"

That question has been asked for centuries.

When a man came to Jesus and asked Him that question, He responded with a story about a man who was robbed, mugged, and left for dead as he traveled from Jerusalem to Jericho. Both a priest and a Levite came by the injured man, saw him, and passed by. But when a Samaritan—a perceived enemy of the man who had been hurt—walked by and saw him, he had compassion on him, bandaged him up, and took him to safety and further care. After Jesus had told this story, He responded to the man who had originally asked the question, "Which of these three do you think was neighbor to him who fell among the thieves?"

The man replied, "He who showed mercy on him." And Jesus said, "Go and do likewise." (See Luke 10:29–37.)

Your neighbor is not solely the person who lives next door or on your block, in your housing development, or in your community. Jesus broadened the outlook to be one of *need*, not proximity. Your neighbor is the person in need.

You might find that person in need at work or on the golf course. You might find that person in the supermarket or as you travel to a neighboring state.

Needs, of course, can be defined in many ways. Not all needs are physical, material, or financial. Some needs are of the heart and mind. Nearly every person has a need for encouragement, for praise and uplifting words, for expressions of hope, faith, and love. People also have a need to hear words of truth. Need is something that is defined ultimately by the receiver. The only sure way to know what people need is to examine their lives closely—in other words, to know them so well that you recognize a need when it arises. Jesus called for His followers to be engaged in direct acts of compassion.

Furthermore, you are compelled by your faith and by everything within you that you intuitively recognize as good to give to your neighbors. Every person has a built-in need to receive love and a built-in need to give. The two are related. Jesus taught, "Give, and it will be given to you," noting that "with the same measure that you use, it will be measured back to you" (Luke 6:38).

To be truly successful, then, you must be generous in meeting the needs of your neighbors. Take a look at the part of your life that is beyond your family, and explore ways in which you might enter into or expand a giving-and-receiving relationship with your neighbors.

■ Your Neighborhoods

Who lives in your neighborhood? Even a century ago, that question might have been fairly easy to answer. People tended to live, work, and worship within the same boundaries. In fact, the concept of parish was based on that principle—a church within walking distance of both home and place of employment.

Today, we have become commuters. We drive miles to work, miles to the mall, miles to church, miles to play, miles to see friends. The neighborhood has not expanded so much as it has fragmented. We have neighbors at work—the person at the next desk or office, the people in our department, the department next to ours, and so forth. We see clients and vendors and colleagues who come in and out of our work neighborhood.

We have a neighborhood, of sorts, in our churches—our particular group of friends or people who serve on the same committees. We have other neighbors, too—those we see at the day-care center, those we routinely encounter at the health club, those we meet regularly in the shops.

And finally, we have our neighbors who live next door and across the street and down the lane.

List all of the neighborhoods in which you routinely live out your life and the key people you know in each neighborhood (those with whom you have regular encounters).

DREAM A LITTLE DREAM:
Surrounded by the Loved and the Lovable

Take a few minutes to imagine that you are at a town meeting at which every person in your community has gathered with the expressed purpose of offering thanks to God. Each person is well dressed and healthy, and has a smile on his or her face. You feel delighted to be with these people you know well.

As you wait for the thanksgiving service to begin, you move freely among the people, greeting your friends warmly, freely giving and receiving loving words and embraces. What do you say to these people? How do you feel being in a group in which each person has abundant reason to give thanks? For what do the people give thanks? Will the people be thankful for you? Why? What have you contributed to the group? How have you served these people? In your imagination, what do you believe this group of people might decide to do as they leave this meeting?

Write freely as thoughts and images come to your mind:

_____
_____
_____
_____
_____
_____
_____
_____
_____
_____
_____
_____
_____
_____
_____
_____
_____
_____
_____
_____
_____
_____
_____
_____

Neighborhood	Neighbors

Reflect on the list you have made. Ask yourself,

Do I know all of the people in my neighborhoods that I should know? _____
Can I call my neighbors by first names? _____
Would I know if these neighbors had needs in their lives? _____

Now identify neighbors you believe you should get to know better. Also indicate a way in which you might get better acquainted with that person.

Neighborhood	Neighbors to Get to Know Better	Means of Getting Acquainted

The Nature of a Good Neighborhood

Most of us have a sense about what we want our neighborhoods to be like. Following is a list of several traits that most people consider desirable. Cross through any that don't apply to you or don't concern you. Then under each neighborhood category you have identified previously, write down the traits that you desire for that neighborhood in priority order (numbering the traits in order of their importance to you). If there are traits that you desire in a neighborhood but that aren't listed here, add them.

Empathy

We speak at different frequencies and think at different frequencies. How many times have you heard people say, "We're not on the same wavelength"? We, in the human race, have been trying to get on the same wavelength for many centuries. It's no wonder there is so much discord in family, social, and international life. Everyone hears a different drummer, sees through a different lens, perceives through a different filter, and decides as a result of a different computer program in the brain. Empathy is the understanding of, awareness of, and sensitivity to the feelings, thoughts, and experiences of another in a vicarious way.

Empathy is "feeling with" someone else.

Empathy is watching the marathon runners at the twenty-mile mark and having your legs ache.

Empathy is crawling into another person's being and looking at yourself through his or her eyes.

Give yourself the following empathy checkup:

- How would I like to have a partner like me if I were my spouse?
- How would I like to have a parent like me if I were my child?
- How would I like to have a student like me if I were the teacher?
- How would I like to have a manager like me if I were my employee?

☐ safety of people
☐ pleasing appearance
☐ free of pests (insects, rodents, animals)
☐ adequate lighting at night
☐ people have lots in common
☐ clean air and water
☐ adequate warning systems for impending crises
☐ places for pedestrians to walk safely

☐ friendliness of people
☐ free of litter and debris
☐ communal recreation areas
☐ diverse population
☐ adequate transportation systems and roads
☐ facilities for disabled persons
☐ community "watch" group
☐ free of graffiti
☐ adequate removal of snow/ice
☐ shelter for homeless persons

☐ places for juveniles to meet and play safely and under supervision

☐ clothing for those who need it

☐ adequate discipline of rule breakers

☐ high morale

☐ educational system for new initiates (among whom are children)

☐ adequate laws or rules

☐ security of property

☐ food for hungry persons

☐ care for those who need it

☐ clean

☐ good repair of individual and communal property

☐ personal privacy

☐ high level of community involvement

☐ adequate enforcement of rules or laws

☐ other desired traits: _____

_____

My Ideal Neighborhoods

	Desirable Traits
Home/block neighborhood:	
My city or town as a whole:	
My workplace:	
My school:	
My church:	

(Note: Your definition of ideal neighborhood should encompass the interior and the exterior.)

My Actual Neighborhoods

Now take a second look at the list of traits and be realistic about your neighborhoods. How do you rank each of the important qualities for each neighborhood in which you live, work, and worship? Identify the neighborhood for each number.

	Actual Traits
Neighborhood #1:	
Neighborhood #2:	
Neighborhood #3:	
Neighborhood #4:	
Neighborhood #5:	
Neighborhood #6:	

Compare these lists to the ones you made describing your ideal neighborhoods. Circle or highlight areas of discrepancy.

My Thoughts and Feelings About My Neighborhoods

Do you like where you live, work, shop, and worship? Respond to each statement with a few words, phrases, or ideas.

Statement	Response
I liked my neighborhood (where I live) more five years ago than now.	
I've noticed these changes in the places I shop and do business over the last five years:	
I'd love to be able to move from this neighborhood.	
I'd change churches if only . . .	
I'd change schools if only . . .	

Statement	Response
The one thing that I dislike about my workplace neighborhood is . . .	
Given the current trend, I see this neighborhood five years from now as being . . .	
If I could change just one thing about my community, it would be . . .	
As cities go, I'd rate my city as . . .	
As states go, I'd rate my state as . . .	
I'm more involved in my neighborhood than I used to be.	

Neighborhood Needs

You are the light of the world. A city that is set on a hill cannot be hidden. Nor do they light a lamp and put it under a basket, but on a lampstand, and it gives light to all who are in the house. Let your light so shine before men, that they may see your good works and glorify your Father in heaven.
—Matthew 5:14–16

In addition to knowing the people who reside in your respective neighborhoods, you need to be able to see needs. Some are individual; some are neighborhood-wide. Many of these needs should have become more obvious to you as you identified what you envision as an ideal neighborhood and compared that to your actual neighborhood or as you described your feelings about the places you call neighborhoods.

Using separate sheets of paper, restate your neighborhoods and then identify *specific* needs that you see in them. Some of them will flow naturally from the discrepancies that you have noted. In some cases, you will need to narrow your definition to a very particular instance or need.

Don't generalize your needs to the point that you have no handle on them. For example, don't state that a neighborhood need is "crime reduction." Be more specific. Perhaps the crime problem is really one of vandalism.

Reflect on your list. For each neighborhood, prioritize the needs. Take the top priority for each neighborhood and restate it. Then state your best idea at helping to resolve this need. Also indicate your role in that solution. You may want to identify others to call on to help you solve this problem. Where and when might you meet with these people to discuss or implement your idea?

Neighborhood Service Groups

Ideally, you have identified various service groups to help you meet needs in your neighborhoods. Some service groups are designed to meet the needs of towns, such as Kiwanis, Rotary, and Lions clubs. Some of them are more neighborhood oriented, such as art juries or garden clubs. Some of them are geared toward service within a group of people, such as church committees or commissions that are primarily concerned about congregational needs.

Very likely, you are already a member of a number of service groups. List them.

Service Group	Neighborhood Served	Focus of Group

In reflecting on your current level of involvement in service groups, go back to your list of neighborhood needs and look for overlap. In what ways might you ask your current service groups or community affiliations to get more involved in solving the needs you have identified?

If you are not a member of a community service group, list groups that you might like to join.

Service Group	Contact Person	How and When to Contact

Serving Needy Individuals Wherever They May Be

Your means of serving others can be through direct contact. Or it might be through a contribution of money or goods.

Note people you feel an urgency to help beyond your neighborhood. If you don't feel such an urgency, ask yourself, What form of suffering would I most like to see eliminated? Also note whether your help is necessary on a one-time basis or on an ongoing basis.

Who Needs Me	How I Can Best Help	Once/Ongoing

■ Your Political Involvement

Greater love has no one than this, than to lay down one's life for his friends.
—John 15:13

In addition to involvement in meeting needs, you—as a citizen of your neighborhood, in a land that has a democratic form of government—have certain responsibilities and obligations. You have a right to be heard, and your community needs for you to be heard.

Voting

Ask yourself the questions below:

Do I vote regularly? _____

If not, is it because I'm not registered to vote? If that's the reason, where can I go to register? Phone number to call to find out where to register: _____
If not, is it because I don't know where to vote? Date and place: _____
If there's another reason, what is it? Is it an adequate reason? What might I do to change this situation? _____

Do I go to the polls adequately informed? _____

If not, what more might I do to become adequately informed? _____

Voter registration is a prerequisite for your being called for jury duty.

Being Politically Involved

Have you ever considered serving your community, state, or nation by holding a public office? If this is a professional goal or part of your current work, you dealt with this issue in chapter 6. This segment is for those who are not politicians by career but who are interested in becoming more active in the political process.

Office Holding

Identify areas in which you might be willing to serve your city, nation, or state in a government position.

Office/ Position	Level of Government	Elected, Paid, Volunteer

Reflect on your list. Ask yourself,

Am I qualified to hold each of these positions at present? If not, what more do I need to become qualified? _____

_____

_____

Have I indicated offices or positions I desire to hold for which there are logical prerequisite positions? Have I indicated a level of government that is beyond my current level of involvement? _____

_____

_____

Do I have a constituency that would elect me to such a position or support my appointment, or is there someone who would welcome my volunteer efforts? (Identify the person or persons.) _____

_____

_____

When in my life do I envision running, volunteering, or applying for such positions? (Indicate time frames.) _____

_____

_____

Involvement in Party or Action Group

In addition to government office, a number of positions need to be filled for each election in informing citizens and motivating them to vote. Generally, these positions are associated with political parties or political action groups. Identify ways in which you might become more active in the political process.

Party or Action Group	Role for Me	Paid or Volunteer	When

Making Your Voice Heard

In our democratic nation, each of us has opportunities for voicing opinions. Check off methods that you find to be most suitable for expressing your concerns and personality:

☐ Public debates

☐ Letter to public official

☐ Letter to candidate

☐ Note in suggestion box

☐ Public demonstration

☐ Making speeches

☐ Call-in talk shows

☐ Attendance at rallies or marches related to issues

☐ Letter to editor of newspaper or manager of broadcast station

☐ Letter to political party

☐ Picket lines

☐ Statements at public forums and meetings

☐ Appearances at task forces and committee meetings

☐ Phone calls to public officials

☐ Phone calls to friends

☐ Paid advertisement or commercial

☐ Other: _____

_____

Identify some of the issues that are most important to you. Next to the issue, indicate what change you would like to see. Be as specific as you can be.

Issue of Importance	Change(s) I'd Like to See

Reflect on your list and prioritize it. Which issue is of *greatest* importance to you?

Top-priority issue: _____

_____

Issue and desired change: _____

_____

_____

_____

What rationale or facts can you use in explaining to others the need you perceive for this change to be made? _____

_____

_____

_____

_____

Now refer to the list of methods at the beginning of this segment. Note the ones you indicated as your preferred outlets for voicing an opinion. List at least three action steps you might take in voicing the need for change that you have just isolated.

Issue/Opinion	Means of Expressing Opinion	Time Frame
1.		
2.		
3.		

When you have isolated an issue, your preferred course of action, your arguments or statement, and your intended course of action (complete with date) and then have carried out that intention, you may want to return to your original set of issues and select a second change. Keep revising your list as you take action to express your opinion and bring about change.

Letting Your Gift Do the Talking

In many cases, money—or a gift of material provision—speaks far louder than words.

The basics of life are actually quite simple:

- Enough food and water for the day
- Adequate clothing for time, place, and work
- Shelter to protect from the elements and to provide safety
- A sense of purpose in life (often a job, role, or function to fill)

Identify some ways in which you might take immediate action to help resolve these basic needs. Your method might be a gift of money to an organization that is geared to helping in a particular area. It might be a gift of clothing (worn, but not worn out; in good repair and clean). It might be a gift of your time and service, perhaps to help build a home for a needy family. It might be providing part-time work for a person or helping someone get job training.

Check off the items that you believe you are qualified to do. Mark through items that you know you couldn't do. Add other items to the list as you think of them. Use this list as an idea starter as you write down the practical ways you might help meet a basic need:

☐ Lick envelopes and stamps   ☐ Carry sign
☐ Speak to interested persons   ☐ Type letters

Handling Rejection

There will be times in all of your relating to others—in your family or in your attempts to become involved with a neighborhood—that you will feel rejected. In those times, it's helpful to isolate the reasons why someone may be rejecting you:

- The rejection could be due to the other person's emotional state. There's little you can do when that happens except to pick yourself up, dust yourself off, and find someone else who is capable of receiving what you have to give.
- The person could be playing devil's advocate to test your level of commitment. If you suspect that is the case, ask him if he is testing you. Also reappraise your level of commitment. For some reason, the person thought you weren't committed. Are you? If so, perhaps you need to find a better way of expressing that commitment.
- The person could be saying no but not really be meaning no. (In other words, you might be miscommunicating.) Ask the person, "Am I hearing you correctly?" Get a clear understanding of the boundaries or behaviors that are acceptable to the other person.
- The person may be rejecting your performance or your behavior but not you as a person. Your help may not be needed or desired *in this instance, at this time,* or *by this person.* If that's the case, don't feel rejected. Just move on to a place and time where your service is welcomed. And stay on good terms with the person who has turned down your offer. She may need you in the future.

☐ Put up signs
☐ Distribute literature
☐ Staff center or volunteer at headquarters
☐ Hammer, saw, measure
☐ Wash, fold, mend, iron
☐ Wear lapel pin
☐ Answer phone

☐ Make signs
☐ Make contribution
☐ Cook
☐ Wait tables
☐ Clean
☐ Other: _____
_____
_____

Also ask yourself, Do I have excess that I can give in any of these areas?

☐ Extra food in cupboard   ☐ Clothing no longer needed
☐ Items or vehicles no longer   ☐ Books or tapes to pass
    used   along

Area of Need	Practical Way I Can Help Meet Need	When
Food and water		
Clothing		
Shelter		
Purpose in life		

As you reflect on your responses, ask yourself,

Is there a way I can involve my family in these acts of giving? _____

_____

If I have indicated a gift of money to an organization, have I listed a specific organization and a specific amount of money? _____

_____

■ Prayerful Involvement

The Scriptures command us to pray for those who are in authority over us—the leaders of our political entities as well as the leaders of our many neighborhoods. (See 1 Tim. 2:1–2.) Prayer for our leaders is a way of having our voices heard in the very highest of places!

Your particular set of leaders may include a wide variety and significant number of people. Cross through any of these that *don't* apply to you, and feel free to add to this list:

parent (or other relative)   board of directors (trustees)
President of the United States   bishop or superintendent

vice president of the United States	pastor (priest, rabbi)
	spiritual director
cabinet members	principal or school president
Supreme Court justices	teacher
senators	coach
members of Congress	mayor (and city officials)
governor	leaders of groups to which you belong
county officials	
president of company	other: _____
vice president of company	_____
company supervisor	_____

Make a prayer list of leaders for whom you will pray on a regular basis. You may want to indicate their position of authority. I suggest that you put the word *my* in front of each position. Even if you did not vote for the person or would prefer to have someone else in that position over you, you are presently subject to the authority of this person.

The list below may be helpful to you as you identify ways in which prayer is appropriate for each leader. You should add to this list any specific things that you know or believe to be needed by the person for whom you are praying.

Leader needs the following:

- Spiritual relationship with the Lord
- Personal safety and health
- Safety and health of family members
- Wisdom and discernment
- Courage and boldness (decisive action)
- Compassion and concern
- Ability to communicate
- Passion for instituting right (in God's eyes)
- Conviction of personal error
- Truthful sources of information
- A belief that a better tomorrow is possible
- Patience and perseverance
- Moments of relaxation and fun
- Fairness

Leader's Name	Position	Need(s)

As you reflect on your prayer list of leaders, ask yourself, How often am I willing to pray for each of these people? _____

Periodically update your prayer list to accommodate new leaders and new needs.

Prayerful Concern

You may also want to pray for the following:

- Nations (their leaders, their people)
- The peace of Jerusalem (see Ps. 11:6–7)
- Specific issues (the people involved in spearheading efforts, votes on specific bills or decisions—whether related to people, animals, the environment, or moral law)
- People experiencing natural catastrophes or crises (such as the victims of floods, earthquakes, hurricanes, tornadoes, fires)
- Christians who are persecuted (around the world, including those who are in prison for their faith)
- People who live in war-torn areas

Ask yourself,

How often am I willing to pray for these needs? _____
Who might join with me in praying about these needs? _____

_____

_____

■ On-the-Move Involvement

Many people aren't involved in community service these days because of travel schedules or frequent transfers. If you travel a great deal or move often, you might find it beneficial to reflect on these questions:

Will there be a time when I am no longer moving as often? What level of community involvement do I envision at that time? _____

Is there an affiliation that I could transfer with me? (Are there clubs or chapters of national organizations that you might be able to find virtually anyplace you live?) _____
Are there issues I need to address in the big neighborhood (national or global) in which I live and move? _____

What might I do while on the road? _____
_____
_____

■ Community Service as a Family-and-Friends Project

Community service is a great way to involve family and friends in activities that can be enjoyable and fulfilling to each person. Note some of the neighborhood activities that you might be able to do with your spouse or a child or a friend.

Activity	Person	Time

■ Summing Up and Setting Goals

You aren't alone. You are continually surrounded by others with whom you have a relationship—even if you aren't fully aware of that relationship and, in some cases, even if you don't *want* that relationship.

Your responsibility to your neighbors includes being aware of all your neighborhoods, the people in them, and their needs, and finding a beneficial way to address those needs and resolve them.

The good news about helping your neighbors is that this help comes back to you—primarily in the form of a better neighborhood in which you live, work, and worship.

As you look back over the pages in this chapter, identify the things that stand out to you and that compel you to want to take action. In particular, note

- neighborhood needs you want to alleviate.
- service clubs you may want to join.
- ways in which you might voice your opinion on issues of key concern to those with the authority to effect change.
- ways in which you might want to become more involved with the political process.
- your prayer list and ways to enact it.
- innovative ways to engage in community involvement with your family.

Summary Statements

Write in one paragraph or less the responsibility you feel toward your neighbors.

_____

_____

_____

_____

Write in one paragraph or less the degree to which you believe you personally can make a positive difference in your neighborhood(s). State your hope for positive change in each of the neighborhoods in which you live, work, and worship.

_____

_____

_____

_____

Write in one paragraph or less the rewards you expect to receive from greater service to and involvement with your neighborhoods. _____

_____

_____

_____

_____

Note any major recurring theme or thought as you filled out these pages.

_____

_____

_____

_____

If you had to write just one word or phrase to motivate yourself toward or remind yourself of the need for greater community involvement, what would that word or phrase be? _____

Goal Statements

As you reflect on this chapter and the summary statements you have written, write your goals related to your neighbors and to issues that involve your city, state, and nation. Focus on actions steps you truly desire to take.

Below are examples of ineffective and effective goal statements:

Ineffective:
Live in a crime-free town.
Get more involved.

Effective:
I will join my Neighborhood Watch group at the next meeting and will push toward the acquisition of more street lights in our neighborhood.
I will join the Caring Commission at my church and, specifically, will volunteer to serve for a year in the ministry that delivers bouquets to persons who are unable to leave their homes.

Your goals can be both short-range and long-range. They can be linked to a specific group, neighborhood, office, or process.

My Community Service Goals

Write your goals related to community service and neighborhood involvement.

_____

_____

_____

_____

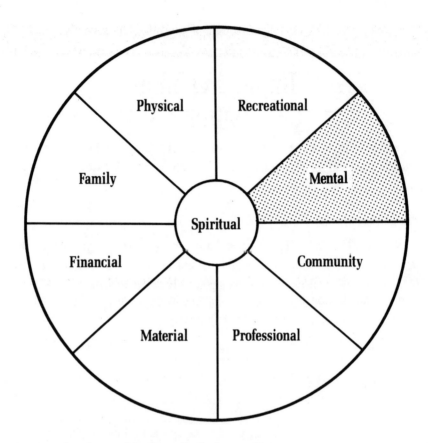

SECRET: What the mind harbors the body manifests.

SCRIPTURES: "Happy is the man who finds wisdom, and the man who gains understanding" (Prov. 3:13).

"For as he thinks in his heart, so is he" (Prov. 23:7).

8

Improving Your Mind

A FEW YEARS AGO, the national advertising campaign for a consortium of colleges had as its slogan "A mind is a terrible thing to waste." That statement is true for all people, no matter their age or situation in life.

The school of life is always in session. Classes never end until the last breath you take. You should never graduate from learning.

Most of us tend to think in terms of formal schooling when we think of education. The fact is, however, that most of our education takes place outside the four walls of a classroom. Our first, and often most effective, teachers are our parents. We learn from grandparents and other family members, siblings and peers, mentors and supervisors. We study a wide variety of courses—from table manners to relationships, from spiritual development to the rules of hopscotch, from corporate skills to the protocol of fishing.

Much of what you learn in life's curriculum is at random. You learn as you go. Other skills are learned intentionally. And in this chapter, you will regard education as something that is best done with an eye toward results and ongoing growth and development.

■ Identifying Educational Objectives

Ideally, the first step in any educational program is establishing objectives— what you want to know and be able to do as the result of a training process. In setting educational goals for yourself, strive for

- Variety. Don't lock yourself into one area of study or focus. A varied self-developed curriculum will make you a more interesting person, will open you up to new possibilities and areas of potential in your life, will acquaint you with new ways of thinking and people you might not otherwise have met, and will challenge you mentally and creatively.
- Excellence. No matter what your chosen course of study or the skill you are attempting to learn, do your best.
- Creativity. Always be alert for new ways of thinking, new ways of using old information, new products, the latest research, the innovative approach. Be curious. Look for ways in which you can experiment or adapt an activity to reflect your personal style or values.
- Skills and information that involve more than one sense or ability. For example, learning to be a gourmet cook involves activities that activate the senses of taste, sight, and smell and, in many ways, eye-hand coordination.

Things I Wish I Knew About or Knew How to Do

For God has not given us a spirit of fear, but of power and of love and of a sound mind.
—2 Timothy 1:7

Begin setting mental goals by listing at least a dozen things that you wish you knew how to do. Have at least one educational goal in each of these areas:

Related to career or job:

_____

_____

Related to community:

_____

_____

Related to sport or game or physical activity:

_____

_____

Related to spiritual life:

_____

_____

DREAM A LITTLE DREAM:
Exploring the Unlimited Boundaries of Your Mind

Take a few minutes to ponder these two foundational premises held by most scientists and educators: the vast majority of people use only a minute portion of their mental capacity, and the mind-power potential of a normal human brain is virtually unlimited.

Imagine that you will be able to learn as much as you desire to learn during the next twelve months. You will not forget what you learn. You will be able to learn quickly. And you will be able to apply what you learn to practical situations. The entire information bank of the universe is available to you. You simply need to make your request, and information will be brought to you in whatever format you request.

What would you want to learn? In what format? How would you feel as you absorb more and more information? What areas of wisdom do you desire?

Write freely as thoughts and images come to your mind:

_____

_____

_____

_____

_____

_____

_____

_____

_____

_____

_____

_____

_____

_____

_____

_____

_____

_____

_____

_____

_____

_____

_____

_____

Related to family:

_____

_____

Related to good stewardship of the environment or material possessions:

_____

_____

Related to finances or money management:

_____

_____

Just for fun or personal interest:

_____

_____

Other:

_____

_____

_____

_____

Highlight in some way the items that you are particularly enthusiastic about gaining skill or knowledge.

Things I *Should* Learn

Take another look at the list of things you have written. Note or highlight in some way—perhaps with an asterisk—the things that you believe others want you to learn or to know. Reflect for a moment on each area of learning. Ask yourself,

Who is asking me to learn this? Why? For what end result in my life? What's in it for them? _____

_____

_____

Am I resisting the suggestion? For what reason? _____

_____

_____

Is the person who is asking me to pursue a particular course of study willing to support me financially, emotionally, and in other ways that may be important to me? If so, can I count on the support to be consistent? What is the person expecting in return for such support? _____

_____

    Also note or highlight in some way the things that you believe you *should* learn, know, or be able to do but that you have very little desire to pursue. For example, some people believe that they *should* know more about investing in the stock market or planning for their retirement, but they have very little interest in finances.

    List at least five things that you believe you should know about or know how to do. Also note at least three reasons why you believe you should know that information or be able to perform that task.

Subject Area	Reasons to Learn This
1.	1. _____ 2. _____ 3. _____
2.	1. _____ 2. _____ 3. _____
3.	1. _____ 2. _____ 3. _____
4.	1. _____ 2. _____ 3. _____
5.	1. _____ 2. _____ 3. _____

Reflect on this list for a few minutes. Are the reasons you have given compelling and persuasive ones? Note the things that provide resistance—the hindrances or fears that keep you from wanting to learn this information or acquire this skill. Recognizing the obstacles may be a major step toward wanting to pursue a goal you previously have been unwilling to tackle.

Books to Read

Much of learning is still related to books—fiction and nonfiction. Using separate sheets of paper, make a list of books that you are interested in reading. Include some serious works as well as books that may be popular or lighthearted. Try to include at least one work of history and one major biographical work. Include at least one area of reading that you may not have encountered before.

Computers, Movies, Videos, and Audiotapes

In our culture, movies, videos, and audiotapes (records, CD's, cassettes) play an important role in education. Using separate sheets of paper, make a list of software, movies, videos, and audiotapes that you would like to view or hear. Include programs that you believe might broaden your horizons—perhaps a motivational cassette album or series of tapes on parenting, a set of videos on a particular subject or theme, or a classic series of movies, or a computer-based skills course.

Events to Attend

Put off, concerning your former conduct, the old man which grows corrupt according to the deceitful lusts, and be renewed in the spirit of your mind, and . . . put on the new man which was created according to God, in true righteousness and holiness.
—Ephesians 4:22–24

Using separate sheets of paper, list events you'd like to attend. They may include live concerts, plays, lectures, and attendance at fairs, galleries, museums, and special exhibits. You may want to include a cultural film series or festival as an event or an event such as a world's fair, the Olympic Games, the return of the swallows to Capistrano, a performance by a particular musician or vocalist, a Broadway musical, a golf tournament, or an international prayer conference.

Places to Visit

A place to visit may be a state or region of the country, another nation, a national park or forest, or a particular building or landmark. It may also be a place that is more readily accessible but that you have never seen, such as the inside of a factory you pass daily on your way to work, the view from the top of the local college bell tower, or a famous restaurant in a nearby city. It may be a theme park or a resort. Using separate sheets of paper, list places you'd like to experience for yourself.

Things to Study or to Learn Systematically

Beyond reading, viewing, experiencing, and traveling—all of which tend to be isolated learning events—you can benefit greatly from a specified course of instruction. In most cases, these will be courses that you design as opposed to enrollment in a college course or in classes at a training center.

Think in terms of your goal. Be able to state specifically what you want to be able to do or information you want to know.

Self-Esteem Questions

Here are six important questions for you to ask about your self-esteem:

1. Do I accept myself just as I am? Would I say that I love myself?

2. Would I rather be somebody else? If so, why?

3. How do I handle criticism? Do I take it personally, or do I seek to learn from criticism?

4. Do I feel guilty when I indulge in some selfish activity? What are some recent examples?

5. How comfortable am I when others praise or compliment me?

6. Do I talk to myself with all due respect or with ridicule?

Don't limit yourself to job-related skills. Include hobbies and personal skills that you would like to acquire. Also indicate the degree of proficiency you'd like to acquire.

Skill or Ability	Degree of Proficiency

Identifying Subtasks

Learning is nearly always incremental. We learn small pieces of information in studying a large subject area. We learn step-by-step small skills in learning how to perform a larger task. What you want to learn will probably become a learning process that involves several stages, steps, or levels of information and skill acquisition.

Virtually all of the instructional objectives you have listed for yourself can be broken down into subtasks. Take five of your learning goals and break them down into subtasks. You may have several levels of subtasks. Pay attention to the order in which some pieces of information need to be learned. If you don't know enough about the area you wish to study in order to break the information down into incremental steps, you may need to consult someone in that field.

Learning goal #1—subtasks required:

_____

_____

_____

_____

Learning goal #2—subtasks required:

_____

_____

_____

_____

Learning goal #3—subtasks required:

_____
_____
_____
_____

Learning goal #4—subtasks required:

_____
_____
_____
_____

Learning goal #5—subtasks required:

_____
_____
_____
_____

Good Advice

You always get what you put in, my child. Plant apple seeds and you get apple trees. Plant the seeds of great ideas, and you will get great individuals. Do you understand what I mean?
—Mabel Reynolds Ostrander, my grandmother

Identifying Suitable Rewards for Learning Achievements

Both students and teachers speak of the joy of learning, the intrinsic rewards of learning something new, and even the psychological and biological "high" experienced in accomplishment. Rewards, however, are usually a very personal matter. What is rewarding to one person may not be rewarding to another. In some cases, intangible rewards are sufficient and may be preferable. In others, tangible rewards are desirable and motivating. In still other situations, tangible rewards may be regarded as inappropriate or even offensive. Your answers to the following questions will give you a basis for determining what you personally need to get out of an educational experience:

What kind of recognition from others do I desire for having learned something new or for having acquired a new task? How do I feel if that recognition is not given? _____

_____

_____

What kinds of tangible rewards are the most satisfying to me? _____

_____

_____

Am I willing to invest time and effort into something that doesn't yield a reward that I find satisfying? _____

_____

_____

Are there situations in which I find that tangible rewards are unnecessary or even objectionable? _____

_____

A wise man will hear and increase learning, And a man of understanding will attain wise counsel.
—Proverbs 1:5

Do I need for rewards to be given by others, or am I capable of giving myself suitable rewards? If so, what meaningful rewards might I give myself?

_____

_____

How do I feel if rewards are given for only partial achievement or less-than-excellent performance? _____

_____

_____

How do I feel when I have accomplished a goal that is meaningful to me?

_____

_____

■ Teachers

Life's teachers may be classified as formal and informal. Formal teachers teach within a recognized educational setting—for example, teachers in schools, church schools, institutes, and studios. A person who gives information on a series of cassette tapes and a person who writes a how-to or highly informative book might be regarded as formal teachers. They usually teach a specified curriculum, with a specified acceptable level of achievement, and with some system of reward. In many cases, we pay formal teachers to teach us what we want to know. Informal teachers are those to whom we turn for certain types of information, usually in life settings (such as kitchens, workshops, backyards, garages, or home offices). We may pay them, and the course of instruction may follow a specified curriculum. But more than likely, the instruction is free-flowing, casual, and without an exchange of money.

G r o w i n g   G r e a t

We grow great by dreams. All [great individuals] are dreamers. They see things in the soft haze of a spring day or in the red fire of a long winter's evening. Some of us let these great dreams die, but others nourish and protect them, nurse them through bad days 'til they bring them to the sunshine and light which come always to those who sincerely hope that their dreams will come true.
                                                              —Woodrow Wilson

---

Name five of your formal teachers who have had the greatest influence on your life. Then name five of the informal teachers from whom you have learned a great deal.

Formal Teachers	*Informal Teachers*
1.	1.
2.	2.
3.	3.
4.	4.
5.	5.

Reflect on the qualities these teachers possessed and what they have meant to your life.

Teachers I'd Like to Have

You need to avail yourself of the best teachers you can find, especially if you have decided to pursue a particular course of study leading to a degree or certification. Don't just look at the school or sponsoring institute. Look at the life of the teacher from whom you will be learning. Does that person embody traits and successes that you want in your life? Does the person really know the subject matter? Does the person know *how* to teach?

Take a few minutes to write down the traits that you believe are important for a teacher to have: _____

_____

_____

_____

_____

Now list several people whom you regard to have what it takes to be a good teacher (regardless of field). They may be people you know personally. They may be people you have only seen or heard from afar. They may be people you know about from others.

Person	Subject	Means of Contact

Reflect for a few moments on your list of teachers.

Have you included experts in your profession? _____

Have you included people who embody at least one type of accomplishment to you—be it spiritual depth, mental achievement, physical fitness, corporate reward, family togetherness, or all-around personal wholeness? _____

You may find that you have listed people from whom you would not learn anything that you think you want to learn, or should learn, or that you have listed people with whom you have no known means of gaining contact. If so, ask yourself these questions:

Even though a particular person doesn't seem to be an expert in a field that I want to study or feel I should study, there's obviously something about the person that I find compelling and interesting. Is it possible that I could benefit from learning what he or she has to offer simply so that I can experience more of the person's life, values, way of communicating, and creative insight? _____

Have I truly exhausted all possible means of gaining contact with this person? What further steps could I take? _____

■ Courses of Study

Courses have direction. They encompass a body of knowledge. They usually require response (in the form of presentations or papers). And they nearly always have some means of evaluation (exams) and reward.

In developing a course—or courses—of study, you need to

- Identify what you want to study. Define the parameters of the subject. You may want to become familiar with the works of Charles Dickens. You may want to hear all of Beethoven's work.
- Develop a reading, viewing, or listening list. Identify five to ten items to learn thoroughly.
- Think about a way in which you can express what you are learning. Assign yourself a series of short essays, develop a slide presentation related to your studies, or write a speech based on what you have learned.
- Choose a suitable reward to give yourself for having completed your course of study. It might be a first edition of a Dickens novel. It might be a ticket to hear a major symphony orchestra perform a Beethoven symphony.

Consider developing courses in various disciplines or areas of your life. I've provided one sample form; duplicate it for as many courses as you desire.

Course: _____

Time frame: _____

Brief description of course: _____
_____

Reading, viewing, or listening list: _____
_____
_____

Means of response to information: _____

Reward for course completion: _____

Are there others with whom you might study this material, or with whom you might meet periodically to discuss various aspects of what you are learning? List them:

_____

_____

Reflect on the courses you have designed. You may want to reprioritize their order or the time frames allotted to them.

Ask yourself,

Which course can I begin first, and how soon? _____

How do I feel after I've completed a course of study? _____

Why is it important for me always to keep learning something new? _____

Have I chosen at least one course of study that is in an area I know very little about? _____

Have I designed at least one course of study that I believe might truly be challenging to my skills, abilities, or personality? _____

Have I crafted at least one course of study that involves other people? _____

■ Summing Up and Setting Goals

What did you learn today? What is the school of life teaching you? What did you need to know that you didn't know?

As you look back over what you have written in this chapter, identify the things about which you say, "Oh, boy!" Which books, events, teachers, or courses of study can you hardly wait to experience? What are you eager to learn? Begin there in making your goals.

Also note

- the different ways you feel as you approach information you *should* know and information you *want* to know.
- what you expect to gain in wisdom—which is the ability to apply information to life in a positive way for positive results.
- ways in which the lists in this chapter differ from your lists in chapter 6.

Positive Self-Discipline

Positive self-discipline is the ability to practice within. Winners are masters of the art of simulation. Like astronauts, championship athletes, great stage performers, skilled surgeons, and truly professional executives and salespeople, they practice flawless techniques in their minds over and over, again and again. They know that thought begets habit, and they discipline their thoughts to create the habit of superb performance. You may have desire. You may feel you are in control. You may expect to go to the moon. But you will never even get near the launching pad without persistent self-discipline.

Most people forget the simple routine for learning a skill or habit: desire, information, simulation, and repetition.

We learned how to walk, drive, type, fly, speak a foreign language, ski, and act in a play—along with so many other skills—using these four steps. Why is it so difficult for us to apply learning to our most important life goals? Everything is habit forming if it is repeated!

Self-discipline alone can make or break a habit. Self-discipline alone can effect a permanent change in your self-image and in you. Self-discipline is the *winning edge* that achieves goals. Self-discipline is mental practice—the commitment to memory of those thoughts and emotions that will override current information stored in the subconscious memory bank. And through relentless repetition, these new thoughts can create a new self-image.

A loser says, "How can you expect me to do it? I don't know how!" A winner says, "Of course, I can do it! I've practiced it mentally a thousand times."

■ Summary Statements

Write a paragraph or less to complete this statement: "I'm a student of . . ."

_____

_____

_____

_____

_____

Write a sentence or two to describe how you feel when you

master a new skill:

_____

successfully try something new for the first time:

_____

complete a puzzle of some kind:

_____

learn something you didn't know:

_____

Write a paragraph or less about the value you place on education and on a person continuing to learn throughout life. _____

_____

_____

_____

_____

As you look back through this chapter what recurring themes or ideas do you see? Note them here:

_____

_____

_____

_____

_____

_____

_____

_____

_____

If you had to choose just one phrase or one word to motivate yourself to improve your mind or expand your knowledge base, what would it be?

_____

_____

_____

_____

_____

■ Goal Statements

Out of your responses and what you have written as summary statements, write all of the goals you have related to learning.

Examples of ineffective and effective educational goal statements are given below:

Ineffective:
Read more.
Go back to school.

Effective:
I will spend at least one hour a night reading.
I will take a course at the local junior college this fall.

The goals related to your continuing education may be short-range, mid-range, or long-range. Apart from your selection of teachers (and their availability), most of these goals should be ones you can accomplish by yourself. Note any goals that require the participation of others.

My Educational Goals

Write your goals for improving your mind.

_____

_____

_____

_____

_____

_____

_____

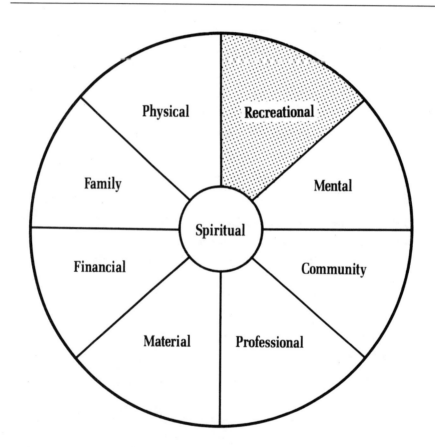

SECRET: To recreate is to re-create yourself.

SCRIPTURE: "Come to Me, all you who labor and are heavy laden, and I will give you rest" (Matt. 11:28).

Relaxing with Family and Friends

BURNOUT GENERALLY results from asking too much of ourselves. We say to ourselves, "You've got to do more, be more, get more, accomplish more"—because in some way we think we don't quite measure up. We fill our lives with activity seven days a week throughout the year to give ourselves more worth.

How do you feel about taking time off from work? What do you find most enjoyable as a means of relaxing? How do you go about re-creating your inner storehouse of energy, enthusiasm, and sense of balance in life? This chapter will give you the opportunity to plan for fun and rest in your life.

Keep in mind as you work through this chapter that the key word to relaxation and recreation is this: *unstructured*. That term may seem to be contradictory to the planning process. Not so. You can plan for unstructured time—setting it aside and then letting that time take on its own nature. You can plan periods with certain activities and people without giving precise definition to those times. You can plan to get away to a beautiful place without defining every aspect of your stay there. True recreation happens only when you let go of task and let life happen.

What you choose to do in the way of relaxing is *up to you*. What one person finds relaxing may be real work to another person. Generally speaking, however, relaxing activities are different from your normal routine of work and chores.

Attempt as you plan for relaxation to allow for spontaneity and surprise. Attempt to build into your plans a big element of play without competition or winners and losers.

■ A Time to Relax

"I just can't get away. I have too much to do." That's a lament most of us have heard, or have made, on more than one occasion. The question to ask in response is this: "When *can* you get away?" The person without an answer hasn't built into the overall life plan enough time for relaxation and recreation.

Thinking About Time Off

In starting to get a handle on your views regarding relaxation and your relaxation habits, mark your response on each continuum.

What I Think	Disagree	Agree
It's very important for a person to find a way to relax every day, apart from sleep.	—+++++—++++++—	
A person is far more effective and productive with a good night's sleep.	—++++—++++++—	
Vacation time is just as important to the quality of my life as work time.	—++++—++++++—	
A person needs time to relax both alone and with others.	—++++—++++++—	

What I Do	Disagree	Agree
I regularly find a way to relax every day, apart from sleep.	—++++—++++++—	
I regularly get a good night's sleep.	—++++—++++++—	
I regularly take vacation days.	—++++—++++++—	
I find ways to relax both alone and with others.	—++++—++++++—	

DREAM A LITTLE DREAM:
Cavorting and Resting in the Good Shepherd's Pasture

Take a few minutes to imagine that you are a yearling lamb in the Lord's pasture. There's an abundance of green grass for you to eat or snuggle into. There's a bubbling stream nearby from which you can drink and by which you can rest. There are other lambs your age with whom you can romp and play. The Shepherd has assured you that nothing can harm you in His pasture—no thorns, no stinging insects, no snakes, no wolves, no enemies whatsoever. Furthermore, it's a bright sunny day with just a slight breeze.

How do you feel in this pasture? What do you do first? What do you do next? What sights and aromas and sounds fill your senses? How do you feel about the Shepherd? How do you feel about the other sheep in this pasture?

Write freely as thoughts and images come to your mind:

_____

_____

_____

_____

_____

_____

_____

_____

_____

_____

_____

_____

_____

_____

_____

_____

_____

_____

_____

_____

_____

_____

Compare and reflect on your two sets of responses. Make any notes about your thinking and habits:

_____

_____

_____

And now answer the two sets of questions below. Don't count hours you are asleep (except in the question pertaining to sleep). Don't count hours that you think are unproductive (such as driving to work). Don't count any hours that have a must-do agenda, schedule, or task assigned to them.

What I Think

How much time in a day do you think a person should spend in unscheduled time (for relaxation, fun, or play)? _____

How much time in a week do you think a person should spend in unscheduled time (for relaxation, fun, or play)? _____

How much time in a month do you think a person should spend in unscheduled time (for relaxation, fun, or play)? _____

How much time in a year do you think a person should spend in unscheduled time (for relaxation, fun, or play)? _____

How many hours of sleep do you think a person should get a night? _____

What I Do

I spend _____ minutes a day in unscheduled time (for relaxation, fun, or play).

I spend _____ hours a week in unscheduled time (for relaxation, fun, or play).

I spend _____ days a month in unscheduled time (for relaxation, fun, or play).

I spend _____ weeks a year in unscheduled time (for relaxation, fun, or play).

I regularly get _____ hours of sleep a night.

Again, compare and reflect on your two sets of responses. Make any notes or comments based on your reflection here:

_____

_____

_____

_____

Finally, respond to these statements:

Statement	Response
Relaxation is a waste of time.	
I don't have time for vacations.	
I'm satisfied with the balance in my life of productive hours, sleep, and recreation.	
I rarely feel better after a vacation. There's so much extra catching up to do at home and on the job.	
I'm not sure I remember how to play—to relax and totally have fun.	
If I spend more time sleeping or goofing off, I won't be able to meet all my goals or have enough money to pay my bills.	

In your comments and reflections, have you identified a need to take off more time for unstructured relaxation? If so, how much more time per day, week, month, or year do you truly want to build into your schedule? If you don't believe you can take one giant leap into a more relaxed life, what incremental step do you believe you can or should take? In one or two sentences, state your overall goal for increased relaxation time. _____

_____

_____

Taking a Minivacation

Many people benefit from taking mental minivacations—five- to fifteen-minute breaks in their routine. These breaks restore energy, renew creativity, and yield new ideas.

1. Get by yourself. Close the door to your office. Go up to the attic. Take a drive in the countryside or go for a walk.

2. Set a mood. For me, that mood involves soft, slow, relaxing music. I love Bach, Handel, and Vivaldi, and I have an affinity for strings. For you, the mood might be other types of music or an environment in which there is a lot of color, or perhaps you enjoy the sound of flowing water or soft rain. Earphones and a cassette player can evoke just about any environment you want these days.

3. Let your mind roam to a time and a place that were thoroughly enjoyable to you or that you imagine might be. Close your eyes, and in your mind's eye, see yourself walking along a beautiful South Seas beach or gazing out at a vista of range after range of snow-capped mountain peaks. See yourself nestled into a cozy lodge in front of a roaring fire or out romping with your dogs as you take a walk along meadow paths. Use your imagination to put yourself into whatever environmental setting is most pleasing and relaxing and enjoyable to you.

4. Breathe deeply. Let your muscles relax. Focus on your hands, feet, and neck. If they are clenched or tight, allow the muscles to relax fully, even if your arms fall by your sides.

5. Picture yourself relaxing, smiling, and feeling great in the environment you have created in your mind. Imagine your ideal self in that setting. Put people in your setting only if you are delighted that they could share such a moment or place with you.

Places to Visit Mentally

List five places that you would mentally find enjoyable to visit in your imagination. Describe the place as fully as you can—time of day, visual appearance, aromas or sounds, the weather, including the temperature.

1. _____
2. _____
3. _____
4. _____
5. _____

Identify at least one place in your home or in your workplace where you can go to be alone for a minivacation: _____

Identify objects or music that can help you create the right mood for relaxing and imagining your minivacation setting: _____

_____

Identify the time of day when you generally feel a slump—low energy, boredom, need for a change of pace: _____

■ A Place to Unwind

On the previous pages, you've been asked to envision a place where you might go to take a minivacation using your imagination. In this section, it's time to get real with those places of beauty and recreation that you enjoy.

Time Encounters

When we were children, time stood still. It took forever for holidays and summer vacation to arrive. A day in grammar school seemed like a week. Our senior year in high school moved at a snail's pace. Our twenty-first birthday was always way out in the future. A Saturday at the beach lasted forever. As we matured, we came to accept that time rules our lives. It's important that we have a keen awareness of the value of time, which once spent is gone from our lives forever. Periodically, we need to have a time encounter.

A time encounter is a life experience in which you come face-to-face with the dramatic reality that there are no time-outs, no substitutions, and no replays in the game of life—and the understanding that the clock is always running. Your encounter may be a near miss on the freeway, the loss of a friend or loved one, an illness, or a visit to a hospital. Your encounter may be as subtle as a high-school class reunion or the discovery of old photographs of you and your family. It may be the chance meeting of an old friend. Your encounter may be an innocent glance in the mirror. It may even be your experience with this life planner.

Those who never succeed are often those who fear the passing of time—and in their fear, they chase time, squander it, or try to hide from it, often beneath a superficial cosmetic veil. Those who truly succeed are those who learn from experiences and develop a cherished respect for the value of time. Those who succeed use time well and enjoy each moment to the fullest.

Places to Visit

List ten places you'd like to visit in the course of your life—not for educational or professional purposes but just for fun. They can be places where you have already been but would like to return. Be as specific as you can be. For example, write "a lodge in Vermont at the peak of fall foliage" rather than "New England." If there are several notable sites or places within your want-to-visit location, note them.

1. _____
2. _____
3. _____
4. _____
5. _____
6. _____
7. _____
8. _____
9. _____
10. _____

Now go back and put an asterisk next to the three places you would most like to visit. Put a proposed date next to your first choice.

Places of Serenity, Relaxation, or Inspiration

Consider some natural aspects that might be associated with serenity, relaxation, or inspiration. Check off ones that apply to you. Cross through ones that you find irritating or painful.

☐ Quiet   ☐ Sunsets
☐ Billowing clouds   ☐ Vistas and views
☐ Gentle rain   ☐ Flowers and greenery
☐ Sound of surf   ☐ Aroma of flowers
☐ Snowfall   ☐ Pristine snowscapes
☐ Bright full moon   ☐ Clean, vacant beach
☐ Placid lake   ☐ High mountain brook
☐ Fern glen   ☐ Hidden grottoes
☐ Bright sunshine   ☐ Aroma of wood burning
☐ Crisp, clean air   ☐ Aroma of spices or foods

- ☐ Waving grain
- ☐ Wisps of ground fog
- ☐ Smell of rain in air
- ☐ Salt air
- ☐ Falling leaves
- ☐ Roaring campfire
- ☐ Birds chirping
- ☐ Star-filled skies
- ☐ Moonrises
- ☐ Waterfalls
- ☐ Wind chimes
- ☐ Dew or light frost on grass
- ☐ Bright autumn foliage
- ☐ Floating adrift on calm water
- ☐ Night sounds
- ☐ Spring breezes
- ☐ Sunrises
- ☐ Moonlight and shadows
- ☐ Birds in flight

List other natural aspects that are appealing and relaxing to you:

_____

_____

_____

Now list at least five places where you can go to experience the aspects of nature that you enjoy the most:

1. _____
2. _____
3. _____
4. _____
5. _____

Here are some indoor or human-created settings that you may find relaxing. Check off the ones that apply to you, and mark through any items that you find annoying or that you would seek to avoid.

- ☐ Sun filtering through stained glass windows
- ☐ Small garden room
- ☐ Cloistered garden
- ☐ Sunroom in house
- ☐ Window seat with a view
- ☐ Cool, dim chapel, cathedral, or sanctuary
- ☐ Room with open-beamed ceilings or atriums
- ☐ Room with lots of windows
- ☐ Room with lots of books
- ☐ Room with beautiful artwork
- ☐ Quadraphonic music
- ☐ Cozy attic
- ☐ Fluffy comforters and pillows

☐ Aroma of potpourri or incense
☐ Bed with fresh iinens
☐ Warm, aromatic bath
☐ Jacuzzi tub under the stars
☐ Sauna
☐ Deck overlooking beautiful vista
☐ Room with skylight
☐ Furniture that you can sink into
☐ Roaring fireplace

☐ Candlelight
☐ Fountains
☐ Massive bouquets of flowers or foliage
☐ Indoor garden or waterfalls
☐ Mobiles
☐ One-person nooks and crannies
☐ Other: _____
_____

Now list at least five places where you can go to experience these indoor or human-created settings that you find relaxing or inspiring:

1. _____
2. _____
3. _____
4. _____
5. _____

Reflect on your lists. Is there a place you can go to experience (in the course of a day perhaps) an environment that has both natural outdoor and human-created indoor features that evoke serenity, relaxation, or inspiration? _____
_____

■ Activities that Re-Create

Take another look at the word *recreation*. We usually associate that word with fun and games, theme parks, and lots of activities. The word can also be taken as re-creation—as in creating anew, creating over, creating again.

Re-creating activities can include solitude, two-person games or play, small-group activity, or large-group activity. Whatever you find renewing is a good re-creating activity.

Renewal includes activities that refresh a person physically, mentally, spiritually, and emotionally. The events build up, restore, and rejuvenate. At the core of this concept is the word energy. Renewal activities restore energy.

Ideally, your recreational activity will trigger renewal in more than one area of your life, although very few activities are likely to trigger renewal in all areas of your life. Seek a balance.

Activities that Inspire, Relax, or Renew

Below is a list of activities that some people find helpful in re-creating their supply of energy. Check off ones that apply to you. (Only check off things that you have experienced and know to be rejuvenating or renewing.) Mark through things that you have tried and you have found to demand energy from you rather than renew energy.

□ Being alone—by choice
□ Listening to music
□ Watching a play
□ Walking through gardens
□ Taking nature walks
□ Working puzzles
□ Hugging, kissing, being close to someone
□ Working with wood
□ Pottery making
□ Sewing
□ Playing instrument
□ Fishing or boating
□ Floating in pool
□ Praising the Lord
□ Writing in journal
□ Reading poetry
□ Working out at a gym
□ Dancing
□ Sharing an activity with friend
□ Working on hobby or craft project
□ Playing golf
□ Playing games with children
□ Reading
□ Attending a concert
□ Visiting a gallery or museum

□ Engaging in sexual intimacy with your spouse
□ Participating in group games
□ Driving through countryside
□ Having relaxed conversation
□ Doing needlework
□ Painting or sculpting
□ Participating in one-person sports
□ Worshiping with fellow believers
□ Group singing
□ Telling stories (one by one, in group)
□ Walking, jogging, swimming, or cycling
□ Watching old movies
□ Window-shopping
□ Sharing an activity with group of friends
□ Visiting theme parks
□ Sitting alone and staring at nothing and letting the ideas come
□ Meditating
□ Other: _____

_____

The LORD will guide you continually, And satisfy your soul in drought, And strengthen your bones; You shall be like a watered garden, And like a spring of water, whose waters do not fail.
—Isaiah 58:11

List the top five things you like to do to unwind and escape from your normal routine and responsibilities. In the column labeled "Dimensions" note which areas of your life are rejuvenated or renewed by this activity: physical, emotional, mental, or spiritual. In the columns to the right, note where you go (or might go) to engage in the activity, and give the date that you last participated in the activity.

Activity	Dimensions	Place	Date
1.			
2.			
3.			
4.			
5.			

Reflect on your responses. Do you have a balance, or are all of your activities aimed at renewal of just one or two areas of your life? In what ways might you plan for a greater balance? _____

_____

_____

Reflect on the possibility that you are in a recreational rut. Did you check off activities that you haven't done in a while but that you enjoyed a lot the last time you engaged in them? Note them here:

_____

_____

If there are activities that you enjoyed doing in the past but that you presently can't do, list the reasons. Then consider what you might do to change or overcome the circumstances or situations. _____

_____

_____

Club Activities

Many people belong to a club or an organized group of some type. Within such groups, they feel free to talk shop, share information and secret tips, relax among friends they see with some degree of regularity, meet new people of similar persuasion or like interest, play at some type of game or activity, and simply be themselves.

Current Memberships

List all of the groups and subgroups (such as committees) to which you belong. (The clubs and organizations you list here should be ones to which you belong for primarily social or personal relaxation and recreation.)

Group	Main Activities	Personal Benefits	Date Joined

Ask yourself about the clubs and organizations you've listed,

Do I truly enjoy being a part of each group I've listed here? _____
Do I regularly participate in each group? _____
Are there activities that I don't enjoy particularly in any of these groups? _____
Do I find that the personal benefits I feel in relation to this group are growing or increasing in importance, or are they lessening or decreasing in importance? _____

You may find that it's time to drop some of the groups in which you are currently a member (active or inactive). If so, note them here:

_____
_____
_____

Lapsed Memberships

Think back over the past. Did you once belong to groups that you might consider rejoining? Are there relationships, activities, or benefits that you miss? List memberships that you may consider renewing.

Group	Membership Dates	Reasons for Dropping Out	Reasons for Rejoining

Reflect on the groups you have listed, and answer these questions:

What time, money, or equipment requirements might a reactivated membership entail? _____

_____

What is the procedure for rejoining or for reactivating your membership?

_____

_____

What particular need might this group meet in your life at present?

_____

_____

Groups to Consider Forming

Have you ever found yourself saying, "I sure wish there was a group that . . ."? Many people develop interests and then discover they have nobody to share them with. Identify a group that you might like to consider creating. Note the activities that you'd find enjoyable. Also note the personal benefits or the possible constraints. _____

_____

Parties

A good party is an event at which people feel totally relaxed and are able to be themselves. Good parties nearly always have a mix of these elements: friends, activity, food, and ambience (generally music or setting).

A Party Attitude

Some people have mixed feelings about parties. Reflect on your attitude toward social events that are aimed solely at group fun:

I am most comfortable at a party in which _____
_____.

I'd do everything possible to avoid a party at which _____
_____.

I am more comfortable being a host than a guest because _____
_____.

If I saw a person at a party who was uncomfortable, I would _____
_____.

If I saw a person at a party who was obnoxious or offensive, I would _____
_____.

The main reasons I see for attending parties are _____
_____.

The main reasons I see for hosting parties are _____
_____.

I like for my children to attend parties that are _____
_____.

I find parties that involve work talk or office politics to be _____
_____.

I'd love to receive an invitation to attend _____
_____.

Best Parties

Think back to the best parties you've ever attended. Describe two or three of them. Note the time and day, location, people present, activity, food, setting, music, and any other aspect of the event that was particularly meaningful or fun for you. Focus on what made it a great party to you.

_____
_____
_____
_____

The Ideal Party

From the parties you described, identify the elements that you consider to make a perfect party, and then plan one. Let your creativity flow as you describe your ideal party.

_____

_____

_____

_____

Is it possible for you to give such a party or a scaled-down version of such a party? When might you host it? _____

Events Now Past Due or Eagerly Desired

Are you overdue in treating someone to dinner, in giving a party to recognize someone's accomplishment, or in welcoming someone to your group, neighborhood, or family? Is there an invitation you should make to return a favor? Is it time for the group to meet at your house?

Identify the event you have in mind (such as party, dinner, reception, tea, luncheon), persons to honor or key people to invite, your primary reason for planning such an event, and the date or season you envision hosting such an event. You may want to review your list and prioritize the events.

Type of Event	In Honor of . . .	Reason for Having Event	Ideal Date

New Things to Try

Is there an activity that you've always been intrigued by or wished you could do just once? Let your imagination wander as you make your list of fun stuff to try.

Event	Experience I Desire to Have	Possible Ways and Means

You may want to reflect on your list in these ways:

How far away do you envision having to go in order to have a truly new and exhilarating experience? Have you forgotten the unusual or interesting experiences you might not yet have undertaken in your immediate surroundings?

_____

_____

How different from your normal routine are the events and experiences that you long to have? Have you perhaps overlooked some slight variations on the theme of your present life? _____

_____

As you have envisioned each of these activities or new experiences, did you see yourself trying them alone, with someone, or with a group of people? Who did you envision sharing each fantasy, excursion, or new experience?

_____

_____

Have you envisioned activities that you are not physically equipped or prepared to enjoy? What might you do to become fit enough or healthy enough to participate in each activity? _____

_____

Go back through your list and put an asterisk next to each event or activity that you believe you might be able to actually do, given sufficient planning, within the next five years. Pick out one or two activities and put dates next to them.

Enjoy the View

Live your life each day as you would climb a mountain. An occasional glance toward the summit keeps the goal in mind, but many beautiful scenes are to be observed from each new vantage point. Climb slowly, steadily, enjoying each passing moment; and the view from the summit will serve as a fitting climax for the journey.
—Harold V. Melchert

Ideal Days

Earlier, you were asked to envision minivacations that you might take on a daily basis. Now is the time to imagine an entire ideal day and an entire ideal day off.

An *ideal day* reflects your normal routines, schedule, responsibilities, and obligations—with all aspects of the day going as planned or desired. Workdays and weekend days can be ideal days. Ideal days reflect your regular schedule. An *ideal day off* is a vacation day—something that is out of your normal routine. It may be either a weekend day or a workday.

My Ideal Day

An ideal day generally is hallmarked by qualities such as those listed below. Check off each item that you value:

- ☐ No unnecessary interruptions
- ☐ No illness
- ☐ Fun moments
- ☐ Incidents that make for good memories
- ☐ A sense of purity
- ☐ Sufficient time to do each task or chore well
- ☐ No tragedies, accidents, or crises
- ☐ High energy levels
- ☐ A sense of accomplishment
- ☐ Personal time
- ☐ Elements of beauty

- ☐ A sense of fulfillment
- ☐ Incidents that evoke favorite memories
- ☐ Relaxed and loving moments with those you count as important
- ☐ Pleasant surprises
- ☐ New ideas
- ☐ No mechanical difficulties
- ☐ Laughter
- ☐ High quality
- ☐ No worry
- ☐ Ease in going to sleep

☐ Good weather

☐ Nutritious food

☐ An opportunity to share things
   that you count as important

☐ All necessary tasks accomplished

☐ No arguments or painful
   encounters

☐ No physical pain

☐ Meaningful conversation

☐ A sense of the Lord's presence

☐ Other: _____

_____

_____

_____

Ideal Day Schedules

An ideal day has a schedule. Create two schedules: one for a regular weekday (or workday), and the other for a regular weekend day. Be as specific as you can be about the activities, agenda, and routines.

Use a separate sheet of paper for each schedule. Account for each hour of the day, even ones set aside for sleep.

Go back and check the traits you identified as being those of an ideal day. Have you accommodated or allowed for as many of those as possible in your ideal schedule?

My Ideal Day Off

Your thinking about an ideal day off should be a possible reality. List things that you'd really like to do if you had a whole day to yourself—a day totally without obligation or responsibility to anybody else. Imagine that this day is going to be on your schedule within the next thirty days. Because this is intended to be a day of pure relaxation, you won't make a schedule—this is, in essence, unstructured time. _____

_____

_____

_____

An Ideal Half Day Off

Let's get even more realistic! If you had only a half day off, what would you like to do? You may want to pick and choose from the list above or identify other activities. _____

_____

_____

Reflect on this list:

What would keep you from doing any of these things on a half day off? _____
_____

How soon might you schedule a half day for nothing but fun? _____

An Ideal Vacation Itinerary

It's time to really pull out all the stops! What would be your schedule for an ideal vacation? You have noted your fantasies about where you'd like to go and things you'd like to try, experience, or do. Now's the time to realistically put together a full itinerary for your dream vacation. This is the one you'd most like to win on your favorite game show! I've provided a guideline for you. (You may want to duplicate this form and plan several ideal vacations.)

My Ideal Vacation

Where to go: _____

How long to stay away: _____

How to get there: _____

    How long it will take to go: _____

    How long it will take to return: _____

When to go:

    Ideal season or travel period for this type of trip: _____

    Specific date (month, season, or year) I think I could realistically take such

        a trip: _____

Where to stay: _____

What to do, see, try, visit, or experience while there: _____
_____
_____
_____

Specific things to take along: _____
_____
_____

Estimated cost of vacation: _____

What must be done to make this a reality: _____

_____

_____

_____

Who might go with me: _____

Memories I'd hope to bring home: _____

_____

_____

_____

_____

Uncommon Man

Crystal ball, O crystal ball, will America rise and fall
Like the Roman legions must, ash to ash and dust to dust?
Is there something more to life than to leave it for my wife
And to give our children more than their parents had before?
I go to work, earn my bread, watch TV, and go to bed—
Sunrise, sunset, year to year. Before I know it, winter's here.
It's not a scrimmage or practice game; there's no Martyr's Hall of
    Fame.
Time, the speedster, takes his toll; every day's the Super Bowl.
Losers live in classic style, that never world called Someday Isle.
They blame bad luck each time they lose and hide with sickness,
    drugs, and booze;
Losing's a habit, so's winning, I'm going to change by beginning—
Live each day as if my last, not in the future, not in the past.
I'm going to dream it now, I'm going to plan it now, I'm going to do
    it now,
I'm going to give it now, I'm going to close these eyes and truly see
The person I'd most like to be. Lord, I think I can, I know I can
Become my greatest coach and fan;
I love myself, but I'll give away all the love I can today;
Lord, I think I can, I know I can, become at last
A most uncommon man.

—Denis Waitley

■ Folks to Include in the Fun

Most activities are more fun if you have someone with whom to enjoy them. Be intentional about including friends and family in your fun and, as a group, re-creating yourselves.

Friends and Family That I Enjoy Being With

Identify friends and family members that you most enjoy spending time with, and next to each name, indicate at least three activities that you enjoy doing together.

Person's Name	Activities We Both Enjoy

Reflect on your list:

Are there clusters of people who seem to enjoy the same activities? Could this be a possible party list? _____

Have you listed events that one or more members of your family *don't* enjoy doing? What about events that *all* members of your family enjoy? _____

_____

_____

_____

Missing Friends

Did you identify friends on your previous list that you haven't seen in a while? If there's any way you can realistically get in touch with those friends and spend some time together, relist them.

Missing Friend	Activity	Date

Phone, Fax, and Letter Friends

Some friends who may be dear to you may live far away. Identify several of them. You have the inventions available to you to maintain good communication anyway! You may call, send a friendship fax, or write a letter. Give yourself a time frame in which to regain contact with each friend.

Friend to Call	By When

■ Summing Up and Setting Goals

As you have worked your way through this chapter, you probably have a basic response to your balance of work and play, and at least an intuitive response to your stress level and need for more relaxation and recreation. Look back through what you have written. In what ways are you

- desiring a break in routine?
- desiring a change of scenery?
- desiring an opportunity to laugh or shout with joy?
- desiring to fall into a long, deep sleep?

Keep those desires in mind as you prepare your summary and goal statements.

Summary Statements

Write in just a few words how you feel right now—mentally, emotionally, spiritually, physically, or as a whole. Don't take time to analyze your situation too deeply. What is your immediate response?

_____

_____

Reflect on what you have just written. What's the remedy? (If you identified a positive state, what can you do to maintain this feeling?)

_____

_____

_____

_____

In a paragraph or less, describe the changes you think you need to make to have a good balance between work and play in your life.

_____

_____

_____

_____

Write a few sentences in response to this well-known statement, inserting your own name into it: "All work and no play makes _____ a very dull person." _____

_____

_____

What recurring ideas or feelings have you had as you have worked your way through these exercises and reflections? _____

_____

_____

_____

If you had just one word or phrase to motivate yourself toward re-creation, what would it be? _____

Goal Statements

Go back through this chapter. Reread your lists and comments. Read aloud your summary statements. Then as quickly as you can, write down as many goals as you can relate to your need for recreation and relaxation.

Examples of ineffective and effective recreational goal statements are given below:

Ineffective:
Get more sleep.
Breathe more fresh air.

Effective:
I will be in bed, prepared for sleep, by _____ o'clock.
I will take a walk every afternoon.

Your recreational and relaxation goals may be short-range, mid-range, or long-range. Although this chapter has a strong social element to it, most of your goals are probably things you can do by yourself. Note the exceptions. What might you need to do to persuade others to follow your lead in moving over into life's slow lane more often?

My Recreational Goals

Write your goals for putting more relaxation and recreation into your life.

_____
_____
_____
_____
_____
_____
_____
_____
_____
_____
_____

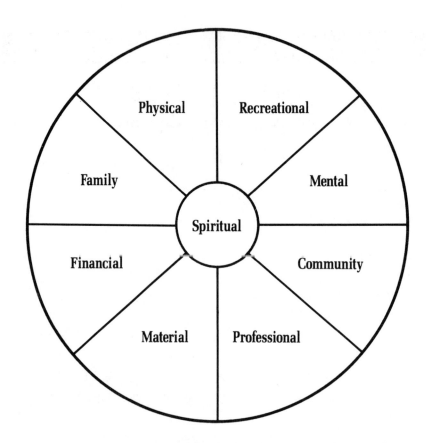

SCRIPTURE: "For which of you, intending to build a tower, does not sit down first and count the cost, whether he has enough to finish it—lest, after he has laid the foundation, and is not able to finish, all who see it begin to mock him, saying, 'This man began to build and was not able to finish'" (Luke 14:28–30).

Making the Nine Empowering Secrets Work Together in Your Life

ALL THAT you have done so far in this book will be of no benefit in your life, of no eternal purpose—indeed, of no consequence at all—unless you forge a plan out of your goals and dreams and put it into action. Success—true wholeness and balance—comes to those who *do*.

James 1:22–25 reminds us that if we are not doers, but hearers only, we are only fooling ourselves:

> Be doers of the word, and not hearers only, deceiving yourselves. For if anyone
> is a hearer of the word and not a doer, he is like a man observing his natural
> face in a mirror; for he observes himself, goes away, and immediately forgets
> what kind of man he was. But he who looks into the perfect law of liberty and
> continues in it, and is not a forgetful hearer but a doer of the work, this one
> will be blessed in what he does.

Take another look at the illustration of your life at the beginning of this conclusion. Only you can follow through and live out the plans you make, and you need all the components of your life—stemming from your spiritual core—to work together. The nine secrets into which you've gained insight can empower you to accomplish this.

■ Forging a Plan Out of Goals and Dreams

A goal is more than a dream. A dream is what you would like for life to be and hold, but a goal is what you intend to make happen.

Goals are intentional. They are rooted in commitment and a desire to do whatever it takes to make a dream come true.

For your spiritual core and the other components of your life, you have been asked to set goals. Now is the time to categorize your goals and develop a specific plan of action for implementing them.

Goal Categorization

Do not be deceived, God is not mocked; for whatever a man sows, that he will also reap. —Galatians 6:7

Your first step in turning goals into plans is to go back to the final pages of each chapter and review your goal statements. Then categorize them as primary goals, intermediate goals, life goals, or new habits.

Primary goals can be achieved within the next three to six months. They may include taking an aptitude test, seeing a physician, fixing the guttering on the house, having a garage sale, joining a Sunday school class, and so forth.

Intermediate goals require six months to five years. They may include completing a college degree or vocational training program, reaching the middle management level in your firm, completing a full reading of the Bible, purchasing a new home, and so forth.

Life goals take longer than five years. They may include long-term career plans, your preparation for retirement years, goals related to a child's future, the building of a vacation home, the establishment of a foundation or charitable organization, and so forth.

New habits are goals that you desire to see implemented in your life on an ongoing basis. They may include developing a daily exercise routine, having a quiet devotional time daily, attending church each week, reading professional journals at least one hour a week, taking a two-hour play break every Thursday, and so forth.

Note all of the goals that you have listed on previous pages.

Goal Prioritization

Your next step is to limit your goals. Look at the goals on the grid forms, and make certain that you have no fewer than three goals and no more than ten goals in each box of the grid.

Through the seminars I've conducted over the years, I've found that few

Goal Categorization Grid

Goals	Primary	Intermediate	Life	Habit
Spiritual				
Physical				
Family				

Goal Categorization Grid				
Goals	Primary	Intermediate	Life	Habit
Financial				
Material				
Professional				

Goal Categorization Grid				
Goals	Primary	Intermediate	Life	Habit
Community				
Mental				
Recreational				

people can mentally handle the challenge of more than ten goals in any area. You may need to cross through several items, combine some items, or subdivide some goals to have three to ten goals.

Arrange the items in each grid in terms of their importance. Keep arranging and rearranging them until you have them in the order of priority you want.

Take as long as you need for this process. This isn't something to do in an hour. You may need to leave your list for a few days and return to it. Study it again. Rearrange items as you want. (A few weeks is not too long for you to take in setting life goals if you've never attempted to set them before.)

You may find, as a very practical matter, that you would like to create this grid on a bulletin board, using index cards, each with a single goal statement. Using cards makes the process of arranging and prioritizing a snap.

Use the grid forms to put your limited (three to ten) goals in priority order.

Priority Goal Cards

When you have your goals in order, zero in on the number one priority you have listed in the primary category for each area. Write out each goal fully, using a separate index card for each goal. You should have nine cards. (If you don't want to use index cards, you may choose to write these priority goals into a daily planner or write them on the back of business-size cards that you can put in your wallet.)

As you state each goal, use one sentence. Keep your statement brief, concrete, and to the point. Begin the sentence with "I am . . . ," and be very specific about your intended level of achievement. Add a date to your goal. For example, your priority goal is to lose weight; your specific goal statement is this: "I am going to weigh 170 pounds by December 1."

Refer to your top-priority goal cards often. Take them with you. Keep them readily accessible. In referring to them often, you will

- reinforce your goals in your mind, literally developing a goal mind.
- keep your goals as priorities despite distractions or obstacles that you may encounter.
- align your daily activities and schedules to help you achieve your goals.

Forging New Habits

Look at your goal categorization grids and take special note of goals you listed as new habits. Review this list to make certain that these are habits you want to implement or maintain in your life on a daily, weekly, or highly periodic basis.

Goal Priority Grid

(Number your goals in each category in order of their priority.)

Goals	Primary	Intermediate	Life	Habit
Spiritual				
Physical				
Family				

Goal Priority Grid

(Number your goals in each category in order of their priority.)

Goals	Primary	Intermediate	Life	Habit
Financial				
Material				
Professional				

Goal Priority Grid

(Number your goals in each category in order of their priority.)

Goals	Primary	Intermediate	Life	Habit
Community				
Mental				
Recreational				

DREAM A LITTLE DREAM:
The Gold Medal Award Ceremony

Take a few minutes to imagine that you have been invited to an award ceremony at which you are going to be given a gold medal. Banners are flying. Singers and musicians are performing in your honor. Speeches are lauding your achievements. The hall of presentation is a beautiful place, filled with the furnishings, colors, aromas, and foliage that represent your favorites. The entire day has been devoted to a celebration of your life.

You move freely among the many people present, receiving their congratulations. You aren't embarrassed, because you know that this award reflects not only your life but also the life of the Lord lived through you.

What are the speakers saying about you? What songs and symbolic elements have been woven into the service to depict your life? How do you feel about what is being said and done? As you bow to have the ribbon necklace with its giant gold medal draped around your neck, you look down at the medal you have been awarded. What does it look like? What message do you see there?

Write freely as thoughts and images come to your mind:

_____

_____

_____

_____

_____

_____

_____

_____

_____

_____

_____

_____

_____

_____

_____

_____

_____

_____

_____

If you had ten goals in each area, you listed ninety things. That's far too many habits for anyone to maintain.

Divide your desired habits into daily, weekly, and monthly categories. If a goal calls for you to do something two or three times a week, you'll need to decide if that is to be listed as a daily or weekly habit. I suggest that you establish it as a weekly habit for the time being. Weekly habits may also be ones that you hope will eventually be a part of your daily routine.

Routine Habits

Daily	Weekly	Monthly

New Daily Habits

List no more than three new daily habits that you would like to implement in your life, and indicate the amount of time you think it will take for you to do each activity.

Daily Habit	Estimated Time
1.	
2.	
3.	

Total Time: _____

Add up the total amount of time you think your daily habits will take. If you have more than one *half* hour of new daily routine, see what you can eliminate.

New Weekly Habits

Narrow your list of weekly habits to no more than two habits and, ideally, just one.

	Weekly Habit	Estimated Time
1.		
2.		

Total Time: _____

If you have estimated more than three hours of weekly habits, reevaluate your list.

New Monthly Habits

Prioritize your monthly habits, and give yourself no more than two new monthly habits to schedule.

	Monthly Habit	Estimated Time
1.		
2.		

Total Time: _____

If you have estimated more than three hours of monthly habits, rethink your list.

Good-Habit Cards

Make a habit card for daily habits, one for weekly habits, and one for monthly habits. List your habits in priority order. Write out the habits in positive statement form, again using the "I am . . ." format. And reinforce your time frame as you write out your statement. For example, "I am enjoying three highly nutritious, low-calorie, low-fat, taste-good, high-fiber meals today."

Keep these habit cards with your goal statements. Use them to reinforce the habits that you value as being important in your life.

Rather than make cards, you may want to write these goals in a master calendar or a planner.

When Goals Are Reached and Habits Are Implemented

After you have reached a goal or implemented fully a new habit (which is likely to take at least ninety days to do), you can move on to other items on your priority list of goals.

Periodically reevaluate all of your goal statements and redo your goal categorization cards. I do this about once a year, ideally after I've returned from a relaxing vacation during which I've rejuvenated my spirit and regained my ability to dream and to see things with a clearer long-range perspective.

Healthy Pride

Pride comes in two varieties: unhealthy and healthy. Sinful pride exalts a person above God or attempts to take God's place.

Healthy pride, on the other hand, compels us to do our best. That kind of pride has a flip side to it: humility. Humility is necessary to know we can do even better.

Healthy pride has these elements:

P—Pleasure	To have healthy pride is to feel pleasure that comes from a job well done or the pleasure of being alive and being you.
R—Respect	To feel healthy pride is to have respect for yourself as a decent, upright individual.
I—Improvement	To have healthy pride is to keep in mind that no human being is perfect and that all of us must work on improving ourselves.
D—Dignity	To feel healthy pride is to have an inner feeling of worthiness, a self-respect that doesn't require the roar of the crowd.
E—Effort	To have healthy pride is to put effort into it. Nothing of value comes easily. Ultimately, there can be no pride in something you have not worked for. Healthy pride is the pleasure felt at work that has led to achievement.

Perhaps more than any other quality, healthy pride in yourself is the key to great achievement.

■ Getting Your Plans onto a Master Calendar

The time has now come for you to take the final definitive step toward turning your dreams and reflections into a plan that can truly create a new reality for you. It's time to put your goals into the context of time and to give yourself deadlines and time frames.

The Daily Calendar

Perhaps you have a daily calendar that you use regularly. Someplace on that calendar, list things that are important for you daily. Include a passage of Scripture, your prayer list, an inspirational thought for the day, priority goals, habits to forge, an hour-by-hour schedule, and a remember-to-do list.

The Weekly Calendar

On your weekly calendar, focus on the weekly habits you are attempting to build into your life and your priority goal statements. Include weekly obligations, weekly special events, the highlights of your schedule on a weekly basis, the week's accomplishments, and new ideas and inspirations.

The Monthly Calendar

On your monthly calendar, include more of the primary goals and monthly habits that you have stated in your primary goal statements. Also note birthdays, key events, major deadlines, key accomplishments and rewards, and recurring thoughts and dreams that you have had during this month.

The Ninety-Day Calendar

This calendar allows you to appraise your personal growth and to identify your intermediate goals. Include major due dates for projects that are intermediate range and events that may require long-range planning (also note things that you had planned to do once every three months or two times a year), goal progress, and trends in each of the nine areas of your life.

The Annual Calendar

List intermediate and long-range goals not previously listed, and identify upcoming events that are beyond the ninety-day range. Note seasons of the church calendar or seasons of your work schedule.

After you have completed your annual calendar, go back and make sure that you have scheduled specific dates on your ninety-day and monthly calendars to coincide with the accomplishment of specific goals or attendance at specific events. Also double-check your lists of priority goals and habits. Have you scheduled each of them onto a calendar?

The Life Calendar

Regard this calendar as having two parts. The first deals with the next five years. Indicate the completion dates of major projects, events that are scheduled beyond the one-year time frame, or major goals you intend to accomplish in something of a sequential order over the next five years. The second deals with the seasons of life. Indicate goals that you envision as being part of a particular range of your life—perhaps by decade or in your retirement. Label these sections by year, if you want, or by a descriptive phrase, such as "current season," "early harvest season," "later harvest season."

■ Staying Motivated

As you develop your plan and give deadlines to it, you also need to develop a means of gratification for yourself—to help you stay motivated and to mark your progress. Periodic rewards give a sense of fulfillment and joy:

- Success of approximates. These are incremental rewards for changes in behavior as you move toward a goal.
- Intermediate gratification. These are brief and uncomplicated rewards you give yourself for completion of a primary goal—usually a one-time or once-a-year action.
- Varied gratification. These rewards are different, planned daily or weekly rewards for long-term behavior changes that you are trying to implement in your life.
- Delayed gratification. These are rewards that you envision as you complete your intermediate and long-range goals.

In setting rewards for yourself, make the journey exciting enough for you to want to take it to its completion, and recognize that you are the primary rewarder of your own goal reaching. Don't expect others to reward you. Reward yourself!

Identify some of the rewards you will give yourself when you accomplish your priority goals.

Priority Goal	Reward

Λ Journal of Significant Achievements

In anticipation of "down" moments, keep a journal of your significant achievements and joyful moments. When you get a little discouraged, take a look at your journal. God can do again what God has done in the past. God doesn't change, and He isn't through using you!

Revisit the Illustration of Your Life

Periodically take a look at the illustration of your life, and evaluate your current level of satisfaction with your spiritual core and the other components of your life. (The first time you do this, compare your results to those in the Introduction.)

	Inadequate		Ideal
	(−)	....	(+)
Spiritual	(−)	....	(+)
Physical	(−)	....	(+)
Family	(−)	....	(+)
Financial	(−)	....	(+)
Material	(−)	....	(+)
Professional	(−)	....	(+)
Community	(−)	....	(+)
Mental	(−)	....	(+)
Recreational	(−)	....	(+)

Ask yourself,

Am I making progress (comparing your scaling to that of a previous evaluation)? Which areas of my life appear out of balance at the present time? Which areas should I revisit to reappraise my dreams and goals? In which area of my life am I feeling the greatest joy?

Growth requires effort, and effort can bring exhaustion (even painful exhaustion). Don't evaluate your progress when you are feeling depressed or discouraged. Neither should you judge your growth and development after a major victory. Instead, evaluate your progress in times when you think you are on an even keel in life, emotionally, mentally, and physically.

Roadblocks and Setbacks

When you are in hot pursuit of a goal or are struggling to develop a new good habit, the last thing in the world you need or want is to encounter a roadblock or a setback. Both are counterproductive to reaching the success and wholeness you want. Still, both occur. Part of a successful life plan includes providing for roadblocks and setbacks. You might call this "Plan B Thinking" or "Providing for ALL Contingencies."

A roadblock is an obstacle that someone puts in your way. A roadblock might be a single action from a single person or a general trend of the culture as a whole. Roadblocks can cause you to lose momentum, but they generally can be overcome with time and effort.

Potential Roadblocks to Priority Goals

For each priority goal, list two to three potential roadblocks you may encounter, and then identify a potential way to overcome each.

Goal	Roadblock	Roadblock Buster

Setbacks

Let us lay aside every weight, and the sin which so easily ensnares us, and let us run with endurance the race that is set before us, looking unto Jesus, the author and finisher of our faith, who for the joy that was set before Him endured the cross, despising the shame, and has sat down at the right hand of the throne of God.
—Hebrews 12:1–2

Setbacks are generally not caused by people, but they can be. They include such things as a major illness, a death in the family, an accident, and a natural catastrophe. A setback can also be a personal failure.

The chief difference between a setback and a roadblock relates not to cause but to your progress. With a roadblock you suffer no material loss. A setback is a situation that brings loss or damage to you, your possessions, your family, or something else that you value.

Setbacks may knock us down, but they don't need to knock us out. Rather than attempt to rebound totally on mental strength, we must, when experiencing setbacks, chart a response that is primarily spiritual.

List your priority goals and then identify three ways in which you might combat any setback in this goal *in the spiritual realm*. What might you do to regain the balance, discernment, energy, courage, and health necessary to move forward once again?

Some of your responses might be among those listed below:

physical rest (sleep)
proper nutrition
listen only to positive
   affirmation
spend time in prayer
spend more time reading Bible
write feelings into journal
let others give to you
find a "safe place" to regroup
forgive offending person
stay in fellowship with others
   who believe as you do
look for the good
let others help shoulder the
   load
refuse to give up
surround self with supportive
   people
focus on healthy habits

put off new major efforts that
   require high energy expenditures
talk to trusted friends
give yourself some time
shore up remaining resources
don't attempt to make major life
   decisions
be willing to laugh again
continue to sing
forgive God
readjust priorities
renew "praise" life
set only small goals for self
evaluate goals weekly or monthly,
   not daily
give up some responsibilities
   temporarily
other: _____

_____

Priority Goal	Spiritual Response to a Setback in This Area

Reflect for a few minutes on your spiritual responses. Are there things you can do now to build yourself up so that you are facing a potential setback with the greatest spiritual strength possible? Do you need to reevaluate any of your priority goals or habits? Make notes to yourself here:

_____

_____

Overcoming and Starting Over

In times of roadblocks, setbacks, or failures, the important step to take is to regain an upward view and a forward motion.

Get your eyes back on the Lord and the big picture He has for your life. (His big picture, of course, includes all of eternity.)

Get your eyes back on your goals you have set for yourself. After you've had sufficient time to heal and restore your energy, reactivate your plans.

As you start over, ask yourself about a roadblock, setback, or failure:

To him who knows to do good and does not do it, to him it is sin.
—James 4:17

What can I learn from this experience? _____

_____

_____

What makes me believe that I can still succeed? _____

_____

_____

Is there any possible good that can come out of this failure? _____

_____

_____

Is there something I'm better off giving up permanently? _____

_____

_____

_____

Are there priorities that I want to readjust as I rebuild? _____

_____

_____

_____

_____

Staying on Track

To stay on track toward wholeness, speak words of faith to yourself. The Scriptures teach us that faith comes by hearing. You should hear from others and from your own lips the things that build up your faith:

- Quote Scriptures aloud to yourself.
- Read aloud inspirational poetry or prose passages.
- Commit to memory and speak to yourself phrases or speeches that inspire you to be all you can be.

In addition to what you speak, take special regard for what you read, hear, or watch. Don't fill your mind with third-rate ideas. Don't dwell on negative opinions or criticisms. Don't harbor fear.

To help you stay motivated, you'll find a set of stickers at the back of this book. Put them on your planning calendars to help you stay motivated day by day, week by week, month by month.

Don't limit yourself to this list. As you see other inspirational phrases (or come up with your own), write them down—in colors, in bold writing. Nobody can be a better coach or fan to you than you can!

What Motivates and Inspires You?

List several sources of inspiration and motivation to which you might turn when you feel discouraged. If there's a particular emotion that a motivational tool has helped you overcome—such as fear, depression, rejection—note that under the column labeled "Good Medicine for."

Type of Event or Material	Title	Good Medicine for . . .

Getting to the Root of Roadblocks

Roadblock behavior has roots that lie deep within the nature of the person who is attempting to block your progress. Take a look at the list on the left. All of these traits are at the root of a roadblock put in your path. The traits to the right are the ones that will get you over, through, under, or around that roadblock!

Roadblock Roots	Roadblock Busters
Unreliability	Reliability
Hostility	Goodwill
Laziness	Willingness
Untidiness	Neatness
Suspicion	Openness
Troublemaking	Cheerfulness
Controversy	Courtesy
Interference	Trust
Dishonesty	Honesty
Selfishness	Empathy

■ Anticipating Your Ultimate Reward

The Scriptures tell us that a great reward comes to those who will "overcome" and "endure to the end." In Revelation 21:7 Jesus tells us that "he who overcomes shall inherit all things, and I will be his God and he shall be My son."

Reflect for a moment on that verse of Scripture. Then write your answers to the following questions:

What things are you looking forward to inheriting as part of your eternal reward?

_____

_____

How do you envision heaven? What does it look like, sound like, smell like, taste like, feel like? _____

_____

What do you think your average "day" might be like in heaven? _____

_____

What do you think you might be doing five hundred years from now? _____

_____

What are you most looking forward to trying when you get to heaven (something that you can't do on earth because of time, space, and physical limitations)?

_____

_____

No matter how excellent you imagine heaven and eternity to be, recognize that God has a better plan! Reflect on the verses given below. What joy to anticipate God's "exceedingly abundantly above" possibilities!

> Now to Him who is able to do exceedingly abundantly above all that we ask or think, according to the power that works in us, to Him be glory in the church by Christ Jesus to all generations, forever and ever (Eph. 3:20–21).

Motivators

Attach these peel-off stickers to your personal planning calendar as a means of providing for yourself a periodic motivational boost!

The sky's my limit!	I will rejoice in the Lord always. Again I will say, rejoice!	My dream may be just out of reach—but it's not out of my sight.	I believe!
I'm going to stake my claim on high—and ON HIGH.	Love is keeping in touch.	No wind blows in favor of a ship without a destination.	Wealth is what I am. It comes from who God is.
Go for the best!	A touch is worth a thousand words.	Have a game plan.	The most potent human power is brainpower.
Think big!	The good old days are here and now.	Keep working.	Happiness is the journey, not the destination.
Shoot for the moon.	The two best days of the week begin with *T*: today and tomorrow.	The harvest is one day closer.	I was born with infinite value.
Make today a joyous happening.	Yes, I can!	Losing is habit forming and may be dangerous to my health.	Thank God, it's today.
I will seek admiration, not attention.	Do it NOW.	Expect the best.	Nice people finish best.
I will include others in my winning.	No one else can fill *my* shoes.	The Lord and I are worth the effort it takes.	Each person has a different finish line.
I will keep the promises I have made to myself and to God.	I am a Very Important Person.	There must be an opportunity behind that problem!	I'm standing for something because I stand on the Rock.
Respond effectively. Reinforce successfully.	My attitude is a choice I make.	I will!	I'm pursuing something because I follow Someone.
Give God the glory and share the success.	I *am* responsible.	The buck stops here.	
Keep the light of hope burning brightly!	Today is the best day possible.	Cooperation is a two-letter word: *WE*.	Life is a do-it-with-God, do-it-for-others, do-it-to-yourself program.